Hands
to • the
Spindle

Number Five:
The CLAYTON WHEAT WILLIAMS
Texas Life Series

Flax wheels, more elaborately crafted than wool wheels, contained a "flyer" and two "whorls." These devices eliminated pauses in spinning by enabling the thread to be wrapped on the bobbin as it was being spun. Courtesy of Gillespie County Historical Society.
Photo by James T. Hershorn.

Hands
to • the
Spindle

Texas
Women
and
Home
Textile
Production,
1822–1880

By Paula Mitchell Marks

Illustrated by Walle Conoly

TEXAS A&M UNIVERSITY PRESS
College Station

The paper used in this book meets the minimum requirements
of the American National Standard for Permanence
of Paper for Printed Library Materials, Z39.48-1984.
Binding materials have been chosen for durability.

Library of Congress Cataloging-in-Publication Data

Marks, Paula Mitchell, 1951–
    Hands to the spindle : Texas women and home textile
production, 1822–1880 / by Paula Mitchell Marks ;
illustrated by Walle Conoly.
       p.   cm. — (The Clayton Wheat Williams Texas life
series ; no. 5)
    Includes bibliographical references and index.
    ISBN 0-89096-699-0
    1. Women textile workers—Texas—History—19th
century. 2. Women weavers—Texas—History—19th
century. 3. Hand weaving—Texas—History—19th
century. 4. Spinning—Texas—History—19th century.
I. Title. II. Series.
HD6073.T42U55 1996
331.4'877'00976409034—dc20   95-46409
                                                    CIP

In memory of *Ruby Fowler Phillips*,
who worked with her hands and with her heart.

Contents

Illustrations

Who can find a virtuous woman?
For her price is far above rubies . . .
She seeketh wool, and flax
and worketh willingly with her hands . . .
She layeth her hands to the spindle,
and her hands hold the distaff.

PROVERBS 31, VERSES 10, 13, 19

Preface

Garments, in days gone by . . . were made by the very persons that wore them, or by those connected to the families to which they belonged.
—Amasa Walker

WE TAKE FOR GRANTED THE EASY AVAIL-ability of machine-produced textiles—of towels and shirts, of suits and sheets—forgetting that, throughout most of history, cloth has been the product of the sustained and skilled work of human hands. Handspun, handknit, hand-woven, hand-dyed—these terms would have seemed redundant to our ancestors, who knew no other kind of fabric. The clothes they wore, the blankets they pulled over their tired bodies, the textiles that furnished their homes were often created in those homes, with women bearing the primary responsibility for their production.

This book explores the last vestiges of that preindustrial, gendered tradition as evidenced in the Anglo-American, African-American, and European settlement of Texas from the 1820s to 1880. In doing so, it undermines two popular and contradictory misconceptions—that home textile production in the dominant Anglo culture died out with the colonial era and that every nineteenth-century pioneer household contained a spinning wheel. In reality, women reared in the old colonial "domestic artisan" role proved remarkably active in home textile production in nineteenth-century Texas, but only until the availability and affordability of commercial yarns and fabric combined with a general waning of the necessary skills to render home weaving virtually obsolete and handspinning the province of only a few.

The significance of nineteenth-century home textile production in Texas lies partly in the fact that it represented a major portion of many a woman's workday and involved her family and community as well and partly in the fact that the activity and the resulting cloth had social, cultural, and political meanings. One scrap of homemade fabric can tell us much about the realities and nuances of a woman's life, of a community's life, in nineteenth-century Texas.

Yet the scraps, whether of cloth or of information, are hard to come by. Textiles lack the durability of other artifacts of material culture; they require careful handling to survive from one generation to the next. And we can sift through stacks of historical records to glean one brief reference to home textile activity. Because this activity was seldom addressed in public records but figured prominently in many a family's life, pioneer memoirs have provided the best information and are highlighted here.

The reader will find a focus on spinning and weaving as the basic steps in textile production, with dyeing as an adjunct activity. Knitting with homespun yarn also qualifies as a form of textile production and was common throughout the time period covered, but I have dealt with it in a cursory manner, as its major nineteenth-century purpose was to produce stockings—necessary, to be sure, but relatively limited. Such home textile activities as quilting, rug hooking and braiding, and sewing and cloth embellishments generally fall outside the scope of this narrative, as they represent creative manipulation and decoration of cloth, not its initial creation.

We should note that "home textile production" here refers to women's working within their own households or in neighbors' homes to produce yarn and cloth for themselves and their families—or, usually on an informal barter basis, for other members of their community. With the exception of skilled slave weavers, who had no control over their labor, only a few women in nineteenth-century Texas became identified occupationally as spinners and weavers, and even these probably did not regularly receive cash for their efforts.

I have only touched on the rich Mexican tradition of spinning, weaving, and dyeing and its manifestations in Hispanic Texas—first, because this tradition had its own distinctive development independent of the one I describe and, second, because little evidence of nineteenth-century Tejana spinning and weaving exists, at least for the non-Spanish-speaking researcher.[1] I hope someone will gather the threads of this aspect of Tejana experience. In women's history, there remain many webs to be woven.

Acknowledgments

THANKS ARE DUE FIRST TO WEAVER CAROL Collier, who encouraged me to delve into textile history. The staff at Texas A&M University Press strengthened my resolve to do so with their acceptance and support of what surely seemed to some an arcane topic. Then, as I moved along the research trail, I met some fine and helpful people, chief among them Cecilia Steinfeldt and Dr. Michaele Haynes at the Witte Museum, Gloria Jaster and Verlie Wegner at Winedale Historical Center, Blanca Materne and Linda Crow of the Gillespie County Historical Society, and Diane Greene, whose 1977 survey of nineteenth-century textiles proved invaluable.

My efforts were enhanced by the continuing assistance of the reading-room staff at the Center for American History (formerly the Barker Texas History Center). I have worked at a number of major U.S. libraries since my first research experiences at the Center, but these folks, led by Ralph Elder, are still the best.

As the project neared completion, James T. Hershorn lent his considerable photography and research skills, and

Dona Price and Eileen Thompson, who regularly put "hands to the spindle," kindly reviewed the manuscript. Textile historian Jane Parker also provided perceptive and useful comments. Suzanne Middlebrooks of Hill Country Weavers proved a helpful resource, and Walle Conoly brought enthusiasm and a skilled artist's magic to the illustrator's task. Each of these people strengthened the project, and any errors that have crept in are my own.

Finally, my thanks to Alan and Carrie, who always draw me so sweetly back to the here and now.

Hands
to • the
Spindle

Chapter One

Legacy
and Contexts

*Every family in the country is a manufactory within
itself and is generally able to make within itself all
the stout and middling stuffs for its own clothing and
household use.... The economy and thriftiness resulting from our household manufactures are such that
they will never again be laid aside....*
　　　　　　　—Thomas Jefferson to John Adams,
　　　　　　　　　　　January 21, 1812

FOR THE EARLIEST EUROPEAN SETTLERS
on America's shores and for those who pushed the colonial
frontier westward, lack of clothing and linens often posed as
acute a challenge as did lack of food and shelter. When meager wardrobes were frayed beyond redemption, when worn,
oft-mended blankets no longer provided protection against
the night chill, what were the frontier colonists to do?

Coming from agrarian and artisan traditions, the European immigrants and the first-, second-, and third-genera-
tion Americans of the seventeenth and eighteenth centuries
often possessed the knowledge necessary to produce ap-

parel and household textiles.[1] In the European regions from which they emigrated, or in the American frontier homes that they left behind, families had grown and processed flax fibers for linen or raised sheep for wool. Most women immigrants knew how to spin, passing the knowledge from mother to daughter. A significant number of women and men had worked as weavers in their former lives—the women primarily in domestic settings, the men as members of European guilds.

But in the early days of eastern settlement, lack of fiber and equipment had led colonists to rely on animal skins when necessary and stymied all but the most resourceful spinners and weavers. Among the most ingenious were New England women who spun "deer hair and even cow's hair" together with hoarded wool, using spinning wheels carried in the immigration or fashioned on the frontier. Women wove "bags and coarse garments" from wild nettles. Mary Todd Lincoln's grandmother Jane Todd in frontier Kentucky was said to have woven her wedding dress "from the weeds and wild flax that were the only textiles available."[2]

As soon as they could, colonists cultivated flax patches (along with hemp for rope and coarse textiles), accumulated sheep as a wool source, had wheelwrights craft spinning wheels, and constructed bulky looms. With rare imported yarn and cloth proving too costly, rural families saw to their own clothing and linen needs. As one historian has noted, "There was a day when a plot of flax was found on every well-ordered farm, just as there was a wheel for flax and another for wool and a big 'barn-frame' loom in every kitchen."[3]

As colonial villages grew into cities, the new urbanites continued to produce yarn and cloth at home. Alice Morse Earle reported in her 1898 *Home Life in Colonial Days,* "Even in large cities nearly all women spun yarn and thread, all could knit, and many had hand-looms to weave cloth at home."[4]

As maritime trade developed, economically advantaged urban dwellers began buying imported materials for clothes and bed and table linens. They gave up their home looms or arrangements with local weavers. Yet spinning wheels continued to be standard in the urban colonial household. Laurel Thatcher Ulrich explains that spinning was still considered a useful and essential skill for mothers to impart to daughters; the work had the advantage of being "easily picked up, easily put down," and it quickly provided yarn for the knitting of small projects, "caps, stockings, dishcloths, and mittens."[5]

Colonial governments encouraged families not only to be self-sufficient but also to produce textiles beyond the needs of their individual households. These governments at various points directed that children and single female family members be taught to spin, offered bounties for homespun wool and linen yardage, and even set flax fiber production quotas for families. From the earliest colonial days, both government officials and entrepreneurs tried to promote silk culture, or sericulture. But silk efforts generally enjoyed little success, although Eliza Lucas Pinckney, experimenting with fiber and dye on her South Carolina plantation, "raised silk and spun enough to make three dresses, one of which she presented to the Dowager Princess of Wales, mother of George III, in 1755."[6]

As the plantation system developed, steady trade with England allowed some of the more prosperous plantation owners to clothe their households in imported fabrics. Perhaps because of the visibility of this group, cotton is generally viewed as a negligible fiber source for home production before the era of the early republic. But many southerners relied on cotton cultivation for their textiles; a Virginia official in 1766 reported women of the colony creating cotton fabric for their own clothes, their children's clothes, and their bed covers. Across the colonies, textiles—whether imported or home produced—were highly valued in estate inventories, "almost as much as silver and land."[7]

Of the three standard fiber sources—flax, wool, and cotton—flax required the most extended effort in processing. Planted in the spring and harvested in the summer, the stalks were first spread in the sun to dry, then "rippled," or pulled through a wooden or wire comb to remove the seeds. Harvesters then bound the flax in bundles and dampened it "to rot the leaves and soften fibres," either by leaving it in the dew or by layering the bundles in a pool of water under boards or stones for a few days. After a second drying came the hard labor at the flax-brake, a wooden implement used to pound the fibers, separating them and removing "from the centre the hard woody 'hexe' or 'bun.'" Workers often repeated this "breaking" process, then "scutched or swingled [the flax] with a swingling block and knife," thus removing the broken outer layer or any remaining bits of bark.[8] After a second scutching, the flax was subjected to repeated "hetcheling," pulling the dampened fibers through sharp wire teeth to remove the short lengths and smooth the long ones into fluid lines. Only then did the spinner judge the linen fiber ready for the wheel—and after spinning, she bleached the yarn. Bleaching often took a couple of weeks of wetting and rinsing and mixing with ashes and hot water before she considered the thread to be of a sufficiently fine color for weaving.

Wool processing was not quite as involved, but it was still labor intensive, involving careful inspection of the shorn fleeces, separation of the coarser and finer sections, washing and handpicking of the wool to remove "dirt, straws, and burrs," and adding of grease when necessary to make the wool more manageable. The wool was then carded, the worker grasping the handles of two carders or "cards"—wooden boards on which were mounted leather insets from which strong wire teeth protruded to catch against the fiber—and "laying the wool fibers across the teeth of one carder," then repeatedly combing the fibers until they "lay flat and straight."[9] This combed wool was rolled off the teeth in puffy sausage-size lengths, ready for the spinner to twist into yarn. Sometimes the spinner dyed the fiber "in the wool," but often coloring was left until after the skeins were formed or even after the cloth was woven.

Cotton processing resembled that of wool. First, processors removed husks and seeds from the picked bolls by hand in an incredibly tedious operation, and then the fiber was carded, spun, and woven. Cotton did not "take" color as well as did wool; dyeing was for the post-spinning or post-weaving stages.

While men were the most likely to engage in the physical labor of breaking flax or shearing sheep, whole families or plantation communities might be involved in picking debris from wool and seeds from cotton and in gathering dyestuffs. However, the latter stages of the process—the hetcheling, carding, spinning, dyeing, and weaving—were generally considered women's work. A colonial woman would spin wool on a "great wheel," also called a "walking wheel" because the spinner paced back and forth while controlling the wheel with her right hand and "manipulating the wool and guiding the yarn on the spindle with her left." If a spinner could devote herself to the task through a full day, she might produce two miles of yarn, "enough for two to four yards of woven wool." Sometimes she took the strands produced and spun two together to create a sturdier "two-ply" yarn. A day at the smaller flax wheel yielded "a mile of linen thread" from an experienced spinner.[10] It took deft and steady hands to "draw" the fibers into firm, even thread, and much of the spinner's success often depended on how expertly the fiber had been carded.

After spinning, the spinner handled the yarn in various ways. For example, she could wind it into a ball for knitting. Or she might transfer it from the great wheel's cornshuck bobbin or the flax wheel's wooden one to a reel or a "swift," both devices around which the thread would be wrapped to form a skein, or continuous loop of yarn.

When women had access to commercial natural dyes (synthetics had not yet been invented) and the money to purchase them, they used imported indigo for blue and madder for red. Indigo (valued for its colorfastness) and madder were also cultivated in some colonial regions; the versatile Eliza Lucas Pinckney, through her experiments with indigo cultivation, made the product of the dye plant "a valuable cash crop for the colony of South Carolina," but she accomplished this primarily through exportation to England.[11]

Most women looked to the woods for their colorings, collecting plants (root, leaf, and flower), bark, and nut hulls. They would steep these natural ingredients with a mordant, a substance that combines with the dye to make it colorfast. Mordants could be items already available at home—vinegar, salt, homemade wood-ash lye, even urine, commonly called "chamber lye." (Children's urine—especially boys'—was considered best but contributed mightily to the unpleasant odor emanating from the dye pot.) The brass or iron in dye pots could act as a mordant, or alum, effective and generally stocked in the rudest stores, could be purchased.

The dyeing itself usually involved uncertainty, as some

While the dye pot held the promise of enlivening drab fabric, no one cherished the smelly work involved.

natural ingredients gave varying colors when gathered in different seasons, and different mordants—or their strengths—yielded a variety of shades and colors. Northeastern settlers used, among others, black walnut, which yielded a generally consistent brown with or without mordants; goldenrod, which with alum produced yellow; and sassafras, which could yield yellow or brown, depending on the mordant and addition of other natural dyes.[12]

Most natural dyes gave muted natural shades—browns,

olive greens, tans, yellow tans—in contrast to the coveted vibrance of skeins dyed with commercial madder and indigo.

After the dyeing of the yarn, the weaver would measure on warping frames or wind on spools the warp yarns, the vertical threads of the fabric. Weft yarns, those that cross the warp horizontally, she would wind onto flat wooden shuttles from which she could release the yarn as it passed back and forth through the warp threads. Or better yet, she would wind the thread onto bobbins or quills that fit into boat shuttles, devices that allowed the thread to unwind freely on its own as it was carried through the warp.

Now the weaver would go to the loom, usually the relatively simple "counterbalance," in which harnesses hang "over rollers opposite each other."[13] Warping the loom involved guiding each vertical thread through the "reed," a narrow frame extending across the front part of the loom and divided into measured spaces by thin strips of reed or cane, then inserting each thread through a heddle, a string with an "eye" in it to hold the thread in place yet allow for movement up and down, as the heddles were already attached to harnesses. With these steps accomplished, she would then tie the threads to the front and back beams. Warping might take longer than the weaving itself, especially if she was planning to weave an elaborate pattern, which called for involved threading.

As the weaving commenced, the weaver pressed a foot treadle to raise one or more harnesses (with a counterbalance loom lowering the others), thus separating the warp yarns. She then "threw the shuttle of weft through the open 'shed.'" By pressing different treadles, she raised and lowered alternate harnesses, each time throwing the shuttle so that thread by thread "the weft yarn was held in place to create the pattern."[14]

A two-harness loom produced simple plain weave, in which every other warp thread is raised for one pass of the shuttle, then lowered for the next. The result was usually the coarse, common linsey-woolsey, composed of linen warp and wool weft. (Later, as cotton yarn became more available, cotton was substituted for the linen.) A loom with four harnesses or more could also produce plain weave, but it considerably expanded the weaver's treadling options with multiple harness combinations. The multiple-harness counterbalance was still relatively limited, in that with it "any two harnesses can be raised or lowered, but they must work in pairs."[15] Jack looms did not operate on a counterbalance system but had independent harnesses raised from below and thus afforded more possibilities. For anything beyond the simplest patterns, weavers referred to a "draft," a diagram that showed the threading arrangement among the harnesses and indicated the order in which harnesses should be raised.

Frontier women collected the Gaillardia plant to use in the dyeing process.

The most popular multiple-harness patterns were twills, their distinctive diagonal lines created by treadling the harnesses so that "each weft float [the pattern of the weft showing on top of the warp] appears slightly to the right or left of the weft before it." Twill weaves produced jean fabric, "widely used since the 16th century for working clothes."[16]

Weavers occasionally used more intricate threadings and treadlings to produce coverlets, "the one piece of home-weaving that could use the more decorative patterning that was impractical in other pieces." The most common pattern was an "overshot," in which every other throw of the shuttle combines with the warp thread to create a plain-weave background, the alternate throws (with dyed yarn) creating an elaborate pattern that "skips" or "floats" over the background.[17]

Although all this home textile activity might appear isolating, it was not. Spinning wheels were portable enough that colonial women would congregate on town commons for "spinning days," complete with friendly skill and speed contests. Or a woman would simply tie her wheel on a horse and ride to a neighbor's for a day of companionship. She could also carry her knitting anywhere, of course, as she could her tape loom, a small device for weaving narrow textiles, such as belts, suspenders, shoestrings, and hatbands; girls took these with them "to a neighbor's house for an afternoon's work, just as they did their knitting-needles and ball of yarn."[18]

The weight and size of a floor loom and the complexities of dressing the loom and following drafts did make weaving a more solitary activity, but informal sharing and bartering of textile work made even this crucial stage in the production of cloth an essentially communal endeavor for all but the most isolated frontier women. A woman wove thread spun by her neighbors, and women from different households took turns on a common loom.

All of this industry was seen as part of woman's role as "domestic artisan," making her a productive member of an economy based in the home. The colonial image of the industrious "goodwife" was rooted in part in the reality that most homemakers processed food and fiber from start to finish—or oversaw such production within the household. The homemaker's performance of these duties attested to her practical and moral worth, whatever her socioeconomic status. Ben Franklin, upon buying his sister a wedding gift, rejected a decorative tea table in favor of a spinning wheel, reasoning that "the character of a good housewife was far preferable to that of being only a pretty gentlewoman."[19]

With the rising tensions between the American colonies and England, and with the ensuing Revolution, home textile production became a patriotic act. Daughters of Liberty organizations across the colonies pledged not only to boycott English-imported tea but also to abstain from eating mutton, thus retaining sheep for their wool, and "to wear only garments of homespun manufacture." Women produced prodigious amounts of yarn and cloth goods in the war effort. The warm woolen "bounty coats" emerged from these efforts—produced in response to the Provincial Congress's plea in the summer of 1775 for thirteen thousand coats in which to wrap the Continental army in the desolate winter ahead. On southern plantations that had depended on imported fabric, "flax was planted, Negresses were taught to spin, and wheels were set in motion" in newly designated spinning and weaving cabins.[20]

With the birth of the republic, homespun became a symbol of democracy and of the virtues of industry and frugality in a struggling new nation, as evidenced by a late-eighteenth-century report from New England: "The Rich and Great strive by example to convince the populace of their error [in seeking luxuries] by Growing their own Flax and Wool, having someone in the Family to dress it, and all the Females spin, several weave and bleach the linen."[21]

Meanwhile, industrial developments enhanced rather than replaced home textile production. Shortly after the Revolution, an American created a machine that "would cut and bend thirty-six thousand wire teeth an hour," making mass production of wool and cotton cards a reality. Fulling mills, using water and heat to create a denser, softer, more uniform cloth, had become "very common" in Massachusetts by 1790.[22]

But the most important development for home textile production after the Revolution was Eli Whitney's invention of the cotton gin in 1792. By this time, southerners were producing their own cotton cloth with some regularity, despite the difficulties created by the pesky cotton seeds that adhered to the raw fiber. Thomas Jefferson in 1786 found most poor southerners and even some of the wealthier class clad in cotton homespun. But the gin, in addition to altering the economic and cultural development of the South, made home cotton textile production much more feasible and common, because the device "cleaned as much in a day as had taken the hand-picker a year to accomplish."[23] Hand gins were soon devised for family use, with more efficient community cotton gins and carding mills further speeding the process.

In England, the great industrial cloth mills clattered to life in the late 1700s, making mass-produced cloth available to the British populace and increasing opportunities for urban Americans to purchase yard goods as well. At first, the British jealously guarded their textile technology, but in 1790 Samuel Slater started "the first successful American" mechanized spinning mill.[24] With strong mill-spun cotton yarn available in the Northeast, some handweavers turned from producing everyday items to creating decorative coverlets.

Despite these changes, in 1810, Secretary of the Treasury Albert Gallatin "estimated that two-thirds of the clothing and house linens nonurban Americans used—and almost everybody *did* live outside cities—was 'the product of family manufactures.'" The disruption in British imports with the War of 1812 stimulated a renewed commitment to home production as a means of lessening reliance on England.[25]

However, in 1814, Francis Cabot Lowell of Boston "established the first American textile factory . . . with both spinning and weaving machines." Industrialization soon altered the old patterns decisively; within three or four decades of Gallatin's estimate, home textile production would virtually die out in the Northeast.[26]

In the Northeast, also, during the first half of the nineteenth century a new ideology of American womanhood was developing. Whereas the industrious goodwife had been the model of the colonial period, the "true woman" or "womanly woman" became the nineteenth-century ideal. With the home factory disappearing, the true woman's chief mission was not to produce for her family's needs but to provide a refuge from the harsh economic world in which her husband did battle and to exert a high moral and cultural influence on her family, all the while remaining submissive to her husband's decisions and desires.[27]

The idea of the "true woman" contrasted with reality for women outside the social and economic elite in the Northeast but especially for women in the South and the West. Through the antebellum period in the more isolated, nonindustrialized South, society adopted and adapted this ideology, particularly emphasizing the refinement and chastity, even sexlessness, of the upper-class white woman. But even for those most representative of this group, the plantation mistresses, the discrepancies between the cultural ideal and the reality of their lives were jarring. As Catherine Clinton has demonstrated, most mistresses had heavy daily responsibilities in the running of the plantation and the care of slaves and family, among them, as we shall see, the providing of clothing and linen.[28]

Rural southern women of farming families continued their home production, and plantation owners employed slave women to make yarn and cloth—often after long days laboring in the fields—when they found it economically feasible to use the slaves' labor in this manner. The slave women's receiving permission to sell their thread sometimes lightened the labor, as did the times when the women and girls had some say in what was produced, and could "stripe the cloth or check it or leave it plain."[29]

Bob Ellis, the son of a Virginia slave woman charged with apportioning and readying the cotton fiber for communal spinning in the evening, remembered his mother moving among the spinners with a song:

Keep yo' eye on de sun,
See how she run,
Don't let her catch you with your work undone,
I'm a trouble, I'm a trouble
Trouble don' las' always.

Ellis explained that this sorrowful entreaty made the women hurry to finish before dark, "'cause it mighty hard handlin' dat cotton thread by firelight."[30]

Some women simply had to work through the night-time hours. Betty Powers's slave mother labored in the fields and cared for and fed a husband and twelve children; late at night, Powers would remember, "you could hear de bump, bump of [her] loom."[31]

Powers's mother no doubt created utilitarian cloth, but home textile production survived as well in decorative coverlet weaving. The "prime period of handwoven coverlets" has been identified as 1810 to about 1850, when home looms produced a dazzling variety of patterns, primarily overshot.[32]

This aesthetic effort was paralleled in the 1830s, 1840s, and early 1850s by the development of Jacquard weaving, an elaborate system originated by Joseph Jacquard in France in 1803. A weaver manipulated threads individually rather than as a group, creating a variety of complex designs within the cloth. But Jacquard weaving required expensive extra equipment and a serious commitment, which women working in the home had neither the time nor the opportunity to make. Thus, this form of weaving became the province of male professionals in the Northeast and Midwest.

Home textile traditions strongly continued during the first half of the nineteenth century on the American frontier. The immigrants who pushed the southern frontier to Mississippi and western Tennessee and populated the "old Northwest"—Ohio, Indiana, Illinois, Michigan, Wisconsin, and part of Minnesota—were primarily farming families used to "doing for themselves." The men made spinning wheels and built looms; the women produced the yarn and cloth. In the old Northwest, lacking fulling mills, settlers had "kicking parties" at which the women shrunk and softened the coarse handwoven material by immersing it in warm suds and agitating the mixture, either with a wooden stick or with the aid of the men, who would jump in and "work the suds with their bare feet."[33]

As members of these same families or others like them crossed the Mississippi and settled through Iowa, Missouri, Arkansas, and Louisiana, as they moved on into Texas or overland to Oregon, women continued to practice their preindustrial textile skills in significant numbers, acting out of both necessity and habit.

In this manner, their lives resembled less those of their contemporaries in the East than those of their foremothers in the far settlements of Virginia and Carolina in the seventeenth century, women of whom William Byrd commented,

"All Spin, weave, and knit, whereby they make good Shift to cloath the whole Family; and to their credit be it recorded, many of them do it very completely."[34]

A long journey to a remote destination—such as to the Far West in the 1840s—required much planning and hard work. The first task for a westering woman was to prepare as much as possible for her own and her family's clothing and linen needs, for both the trip itself and the new location. Iowa resident Kitturah Belknap worked industriously through the winter of 1847–48 to ready for the trip to Oregon, as such journal entries as the following demonstrate:

> The first thing is to make a piece of linen for a wagon cover and some sacks. Will spin mostly evenings while my husband reads to me. The little wheel in the corner doesn't make any noise. I spin for Mother Belknap [her mother-in-law] and Mrs. Hawley and they will weave. Now that it [the warp] is in the loom I must work almost day and night to get the filling ready to keep the loom busy.[35]

Belknap also spun the thread for clothes for her family and referred to homemade flour sacks, which she probably helped produce. Because of communal effort, she did not weave, but she did cut and hand sew everything of her family's that came from the loom.

Another midwestern family, the Thompsons, demonstrated the level of communal activity involved in their 1852 overland journey preparations: "Every article of wearing apparel must be made at home. 'Store clothes' were out of the question in those days. Wool must be carded and spun into thread for Aunt Ann's old wooden loom. The cloth was then fashioned into garments for clothing to last a year after we should reach our goal far out on the Pacific shores. The crank of the old wooden loom was almost ceaseless. Merrily the shuttle sang to an accompaniment of a camp meeting melody. Neighbors also volunteered their services in weaving and fashioning garments for the family. All was bustle and hurry."[36]

Families tried to pack the tools necessary for cloth production in their new environments. A pair of knitting needles and yarn were easily carried, and many a female immigrant knitted her way westward, plying her needles from a wagon seat.[37] Looms, even dismantled, were too unwieldy for all but the most determined. Families packed spinning wheels in westward-bound wagons; some had even been carried across the Atlantic by European emigrants. Some travelers carried raw wool or cotton or ready-to-spin flax.

To their sorrow, the families often jettisoned many of the supplies along hard trails. Meanwhile, clothing and linens frayed and wore—and sometimes were relinquished altogether. "We sewed her up in a sheet and a quilt," one Utah immigrant recalled of the cholera death of a member of her party on the Platte River. "That was all that could be done for her burial."[38]

As had their frontier predecessors, nineteenth-century immigrants at journey's end found themselves lacking not only clothing and linens but also the fibers and tools to supply them. Again, animal skins, primarily buckskin, became common clothing, particularly for men and boys. In the old Northwest, spinners combined buffalo wool or bear's fur with milkweed or wild nettle and managed to produce a rough yarn. One early immigrant to Oregon recalled similar attempts with wolf hair: "It was a poor substitute [for wool], for the yarn spun of it was coarse and not strong. Another drawback was that wolves could not be fleeced so long as they were alive, and a man could not kill a sufficient number of the kind that were common, the prairie wolf or coyote, in a month, to make a sweater.

The yarn spun from the fleece of one pelt would hardly make a pair of slippers for a child."[39]

On the southern and midwestern frontiers, families planted flax and cotton patches and began to raise sheep. David Anders's memory of his childhood in Arkansas in the second and third decades of the nineteenth century illustrate this transitional period: "We dressed like the Indians; we did not wear much clothes; we raised our flax, and worked it into cloth, and cloth clothes, in those days were made of flax. I can recollect wearing a long flax shirt till I was twelve years old. My first pants were made of dressed deer skin."[40]

Gradually commercial dyes, even commercial wheels and looms, became available. Inevitably, these same supply networks made affordable cloth available as well. As each frontier area settled into a more established phase, women abandoned the spinning wheel, loom, and dye pot. They poured their home textile energies into cutting and sewing store-bought cloth.

Still, we can find numerous examples of home cloth production in the trans-Mississippi West, including on the Texas frontier, right up to the beginning of the Civil War.[41] Then, with the disruption of supply lines and the channeling of resources into the war effort, most Southerners and some Northerners found themselves in the cloth-poor situation of their colonial forebears and their frontier contemporaries. Southern plantation owners "convert[ed] their homes to [cloth] manufacturing centers." Women who had long ago retired their spinning wheels pulled them from dusty attics; women who had never before had need to learn spinning and weaving endeavored to learn in order to clothe their families and their fighting men and "to produce linen and bandages for hospitals."[42]

Meanwhile, frontier women continued to ply their textile skills, war or no war. Mary Jane McCurdy, who grew up in Arkansas and Texas in the late 1850s and 1860s, would recall, "I can remember only one time when Ma went to town and bought us a calico dress while we were kids. We wove everything we wore and all our sheets, table cloths, blankets and bed spreads."[43]

After the war, a number of factors combined to end the "age of homespun" for most Americans. Most significantly, supply routes in the South and West were reopened and improved, and inexpensive factory-produced textiles flooded into all but the most remote regions.

Yet many women continued to spin thread for hand knitting, and those from isolated areas of the East to the Far West continued to spin and weave. In the Appalachian Mountains in the late nineteenth century, women kept alive the coverlet tradition—processing home-grown flax, carding wool from family sheep, searching the hills for dyestuffs, and producing intricately woven bed covers for gift-giving, sale, and barter.[44] In the Arkansas Ozarks in the 1880s women continued the home production of wool thread for the knitting of stockings, mittens, and wristbands, the last "worn . . . by men to supplement the gloves and keep their wrists warm," and for the home loom, with which they produced blankets and material for women's dresses and men's suits.[45]

Full home production thrived in some areas of the trans-Mississippi region in the 1870s and 1880s. In Utah, Mormon pioneer women proved their self-sufficiency by successfully raising silkworms "at home on wooden frames strung with twine," after which they "boiled, reeled, spun, and wove" silk fabrics. While silkworm raising, an involved task, required the women to carry the mulberry leaves to the worms "around the clock for the twenty to twenty-two days of their eating life," one woman nonetheless dryly judged it "not too much trouble, as [the worms] did not require their food cooked."[46]

As in Appalachia, women in other relatively isolated regions continued in the old traditions of self-sufficiency, as in the Big Thicket of Texas. Others continued to practice the skills they had learned as children or young matrons, whether or not the activity was common to the region. Elmey Sammis Trimmer, who emigrated from New York to Ohio in 1839, generated income from her weaving until the 1870s. Malinda Jenkins, whose third child was born in Indiana in the 1870s, "in the fall and winter before" the birth "spun and wove four blankets," sewed all the family clothes, knitted stockings, and as she neared her due date, wove a rag rug "with the breastpiece of the loom rubbing against me, and a grease cloth tied around my stomach to keep it from hurting."[47]

Jenkins felt pride in her ability and self-reliance, a pride reflected in the textile experiences and accomplishments of many westering women who settled in nineteenth-century Texas. Like their predecessors in the East, like their sisters in the West, these women imbued with personal and broader meanings their hand-spinning, weaving, and dyeing.

They were not, however, the first Texans to do so. Native American, Spanish, and Mexican textile production long preceded Anglo-American activity. In fact, native production can be traced back as far as 200 A.D., for extant from this period in Texas prehistory is a fragment of a blanket or cape with a plant-fiber warp and a weft composed of strips of rabbit skin. Yet by the time the Spanish established their presence in the 1700s, they knew the natives "only for various knotting and basketry techniques," with their clothing made from "prepared animal skins."[48]

Spanish priests put the natives to work spinning and weaving in their Texas missions during the eighteenth century. Despite the fact that early Spanish explorers found flax growing wild in Texas, wool and cotton seem to have been the fibers of choice, with the wool obtained from mission herds and the cotton from mission farms. Native women, youths, and children provided the labor force that washed the wool and spun; as with production in the English colonies, sometimes the wool was spun twice—once by the children and youths and again, as plied yarn, by the women. Children also spun cotton.

Spinners met daily quotas. They took the yarn to the *obraje,* or mission weaving room, where two or three looms stood ready, and native weavers produced material of "a regular width to make clothing for adults and a narrower one for children's clothing and to distribute to the poor." They also turned out "bedclothes, including cotton and wool blankets, quilts, sheets, pillowcases, and other items such as tablecloths, napkins, and towels."[49]

The San Antonio missions in particular employed many busy textile workers in the mid-eighteenth century, but cloth produced by Mexican professionals and even European and Asian fabrics had been available in Mexico for a long time and was also available to mission personnel and colonizers. In 1729, the mission Nuestra Señora del Espíritu Santo de Zúñiga at Goliad had on hand such goods as "shawls, blankets, and cloth woven in Mexico" and "silk, fine woolen, brocade, linen, and cotton shirting from England, France, Italy, Spain and China as well as silk and worsted stockings from England, Spain, Italy, France and Holland." A soldier, Miguel de Castro, who settled in San Antonio prior to 1731, included a loom among the possessions in his will, but records show that he and his wife bestowed upon their adolescent daughters silks and gauze, such luxury items perhaps obtained "through contraband trade with the French in Louisiana."[50]

When Anglo settlers arrived in Texas in the 1820s, female Mexican colonists were apparently still spinning and weaving, as were their contemporaries in rural areas of Mexico. Noah Smithwick wrote of these Mexican women using drop spindles, simple winding devices that required quite a bit of dexterity, to twist wool into yarn, and then weaving the yarn into blankets on simple frame looms. These looms lacked harnesses to raise the warp threads, so for each pass of the weft thread, the weaver manipulated the warp threads manually, sliding a board between those to go up and those to go down, then turning the board to open the "shed" for the weft yarn to be inserted.[51]

A professional Mexican weaving tradition had developed along the border; an 1822 census listed 131 weavers in El Paso.[52] But it appears that Mexican supply lines provided most Hispanic occupants of Texas with fabrics, trade in general being stimulated by the rapid development of the Santa Fe Trail in the early 1820s.

Interestingly, by this time "isolated examples of loom weaving among the Indians of Texas and trading for woven woolen blankets and cloaks with the Navajo Indians in New Mexico" also existed. The Cherokees who had begun immigrating into Texas from the South in 1819 "had been growing cotton since the late eighteenth century," devising their own looms and obtaining spinning wheels and cotton cards from the United States government. In Texas they planted cotton, and the women used the cloth they produced for barter with the established Hispanic settlers and the Anglo newcomers.[53]

The idea of natives, Hispanic weavers, and early Anglo settlers exchanging textile techniques and modifying their own product through cross-cultural influence is an enticing one, but fragmentary records provide virtually no support for such an interweaving of cultural traditions.[54] The settlers from the United States who began arriving in the early 1820s were overwhelmingly Americans of northern European origin from the South and were increasingly accompanied by African-American slaves. The traditions they brought to Texas accordingly reflected those of the eastern United States, particularly the middle and deep South.

The arrival of these settlers signaled an era of extended home textile production in Texas. This era can be divided into three distinct time periods: early colonization (1822–36), when most women and families brought textile production skills westward and many used them; expansion and continuation of the frontier (1836–60), when home textile production dwindled in more established areas but continued a vital tradition on the widening western frontier; and war and change (1860–80), when home textile production again became necessary for most families and communities across the state and then diminished with the wide availability of inexpensive fabrics.

In each period, the hum of the spinning wheel and the clatter of the loom provided a regular accompaniment to the lives of many a westering Texas woman and her family. What follows are the stories of these women and families as makers of cloth.

Chapter
Two

❦

The Early Years,
1822–1836

*It is found easier to raise or manufacture such ar-
ticles as are needed in a family, rough and clumsy as
they may be, or to do without, than to obtain them
from abroad, or employ an individual to scour the
country in search of such as may be desired.*

—David Edward, *in his*
1836 Texas immigrants' guide

THE ERA OF ANGLO SETTLEMENT IN TEXAS
began with the arrival of colonists in 1822, as empresario
Stephen F. Austin labored to win from the newly independent Mexican government a grant on which to locate them.
At the time, Texas was simply a northern Mexican province, its distances, geography, and native inhabitants having combined to impede Spanish and Mexican settlement
and development. Austin succeeded in his initial quest in
1823, gaining permission to establish a colony of three
hundred carefully selected families from the United States

along the coastal prairies, inland timberlands, and black-land prairies of southeastern Texas.

An astute and sensitive leader, Austin championed the use of homespun in the colony, echoing the eighteenth-century New England themes of industry, frugality, and democracy. He would write of his desire for "*economy* and *plain* living" in a letter to his mother and sister: "It is my wish that nothing should be worn in the family but homespun, at least for several years it is the cheapest but what is of more importance it will set an example to the rest of the settlers that will have a very good effect . . . we are all poor in this country and therefore all on an equality and so long as this continues we shall all go on well and harmoniously. . . ."[1]

Some felt uneasy with the change in women's labor roles when mass-produced fabrics became available. Just as "male, upper-class observers" in the American Northeast voiced the fear that "farm wives and daughters would have empty time on their hands," so a poem printed in the Austin colony newspaper, the San Felipe de Austin *Texas Gazette* of January 30, 1830, contrasted the female activity of the past—"Our mothers nurtured to the nodding reel/ Gave all their daughters lessons on the wheel"—to the "unnatural and luxurious present times" in which "damsels" guarded their fingernails and "sought . . . gaudy dress."[2]

Tied to this concern was a palpable nostalgia for a traditional way of life threatened by urbanization and industrialization. The article accompanying the *Texas Gazette* poem extolled the pleasures of a "snug little farm" and a wife "that can discourse music on the cheerful spinning wheel."

The idea that women would have less to do when no longer charged with textile production would turn out to be absurd, as they continued to face a demanding range of tasks within the home and extended their sewing activity using manufactured fabrics.³ And the nostalgia for agrarian life and the spinning wheel, as appropriate as it might have been in the 1820s in the urbanizing and industrializing Northeast, was definitely premature in agrarian Texas. Other empresarios followed Austin's lead, establishing their own colonies, but frontier conditions prevailed for all. Although Austin's directive to his female relatives indicates that home-spun was less a necessity than a thrifty choice for some, the music of the spinning wheel would continue to accompany westward migration for half a century to come.

As did their contemporaries bound for Missouri and Iowa—and later for the Far West—some Texas immigrant women tried to dispense with the need for spinning wheel and loom—at least for a long period—by working fever-ishly on textile production before departure and by pack-ing carefully. Harriet Duke Cole, preparing to move to the old East Texas Spanish outpost of Nacogdoches about the time Austin instituted his colony, spun and wove in her South Carolina home, producing family clothing, house-hold linens, and even beautifully designed counterpanes to take with her. Sarah Wade Brown of Tennessee, who moved to Sterling Robertson's colony north of Austin's in 1835, packed linens and flannels along with medicines, conscious that "the move meant for her the breaking of all hope to supply herself with these things."⁴

The earliest Anglo female settlers came overwhelmingly as members of rural southern farming families and, as such, retained the textile production knowledge that had served their mothers and grandmothers. As an early twentieth-century memorialist wrote of Laura Metz Marshall-Flack, a South Carolinian born in 1826 who moved to Texas as a child, "she could sew and knit, spin and weave, could do, in short, anything that a girl of her day and circumstances was required to do."[5]

Some women during this period came as members of southern plantation aristocracy, as small slaveholders, or as slaves; for mistress and slave alike, the need to produce cheap clothing for plantation workers and the need or gendered cultural aesthetic to spin and weave fine cloth and linens for the plantation family often occasioned some knowledge of home textile production.

At first, however, just as on the eastern frontier, many settlers lacked the tools and fiber necessary to produce cloth. Some attempted to carry these items with them; for example, the Yoast family of Virginia loaded flax and a spinning wheel when they set out for Texas. But after a difficult journey, and an extended stay in Alabama, they are reported arriving with one wagon, bedding, and cooking pots.

Nowhere is the lack of equipment and fiber demonstrated more directly than in the memoirs of Noah Smithwick, the youthful adventurer who visited Green Dewitt's colony to the west of Austin's in the late 1820s. Women colonists "talked sadly of the old homes and friends left behind . . . of the hardships and bitter privations they were undergoing and the dangers that surrounded them. They had not even the solace of constant employment. The spinning wheel and loom had been left behind. There was, as yet, no use for them—there was nothing to spin."[6]

While spinning and weaving are presented here as a way to break the monotony of an isolated and precarious existence, women almost invariably undertook these activities only when necessary. Early Anglo Texans often found themselves ill-supplied with linens and ill-clothed, perhaps reduced to one badly worn outfit. For the African-American slaves brought westward by some of the colonists, their clothing needs had usually been poorly met to begin with, leaving them in even greater want.

This portrait is not meant to suggest that all westering immigrants to Texas in the Mexican period had no choices beyond what they or members of their family or community could produce. G. Logan, taking care of business for Texas merchant and plantation owner James Franklin Perry at Brazoria in December, 1832, wrote, "Your Wool cards that I left at Hodges are there yet it seems as if you have no use for them."[7] Those who settled around the coastal ports quickly had ready access to dry goods from New Orleans; those who moved up the Brazos River into Austin's well-settled colony, if they did not go too far, soon found supply lines established. The *Texas Gazette* in 1830 carried ads offering muslins and calicoes, tailor services, even ready-made clothing, although the last was often hard for merchants to obtain. Owners established their plantations along natural supply lines (rivers, East Texas routes), and some were soon able to order from afar the coarse "negro cloth" that had provided staple slave clothing for decades.

But as settlement began to fan northwestward, most male Texas immigrants, like their forebears, turned to animal skins, specifically buckskin. More than homespun, buckskin seemed to symbolize a rude masculine equality and pride in one's frontier existence. Sam Houston was known to favor buckskin attire even over available alternatives. One correspondent to the *Texas Gazette*, "An Old Kentuckian," commented on good Texas prospects for growing hemp, which could be used to produce a rough cloth as well as rope, but concluded, "For comfortable and lasting apparel, give me the well dressed Texas buckskin in preference to all the ROTTED hemp in Kentucky!!!!!!!!!!"[8]

Pioneer accounts researched make no mention of women and girls wearing buckskin, except for buckskin moccasins, although one 1844 account of early settlers on the Brazos notes that they "had fashioned their clothing and shoes of deerskin" until peddlers appeared with "bullets, cotton cloth, cooking utensils, and salt, and sometimes coffee too."[9] Women probably "foxed"—used buckskin patches on—their own garments as well as men's, but gender distinctions seemed to dictate that women wear homespun or calico, even if that meant that women's primary textile activity served themselves rather than the male members of the family.

Such activity may appear in direct contradiction to the model of the self-sacrificing "helpmate" of American womanhood, but women were involved in producing buckskin clothing for the men as well. Further, standards of female propriety, including, perhaps, a cultural uneasiness in associating women with wild animals, must have played a large part in creating the distinction.

At any rate, families soon began cultivating cotton and raising sheep, and women worked not only to clothe themselves but also to provide for their families. One of the most charming of frontier chroniclers, Mary Crownover Rabb, with her husband John located in a log house in Austin's colony in 1823 near the present site of La Grange: "I was in my first Texas house, and [brother-in-law] Andrew Rabb made a spinning wheel and made me a present of it. I was very much pleased, and I soon got to work to make clothing for my family." Mary Rabb's autobiographical narrative demonstrates matter-of-factly the extent and significance of one early frontier woman's textile-producing activity. When John left on a ten-day trip to claim his headright, leaving Mary alone with their first baby, she blotted out the presence and threat of Indians by keeping "my new spinning wheel whistling all day and a good part of the night, for while the wheel was roaring, it would keep me from hearing the Indians walking around hunting mischief."[10]

When the peripatetic Rabbs moved on, the spinning wheel accompanied them, two chickens tied to it, and the wheel itself tied to their pony Nickety Poly. Whenever they stopped at a location and considered staying, Mary set to spinning. On the Brazos River, "We put up a quilt and a sheet for a tent. I got the head of my wheel under the tent. I got to spinning again."[11]

After a further move to the Bernard River, John left again, "to burn off a canebrake" on the Colorado River, and was gone all summer. Now with two small children, Mary reported, "I would pick the cotton with my fingers and spin six hundred thread around the reel every day and milk my cows and pound my meal in a mortar and cook and churn and mind my children."[12]

When the Rabbs moved to their headright, John made Mary a partial shelter for spinning—"a camp . . . covered with . . . boards"—and a loom. After prodigious spinning, Mary wove forty-six yards of mosquito netting and an un-specified length of cloth "in the open air and sun" *before* John constructed a house and loom shed. They had not been in the house long before John "took a notion that he could not stay there as we had no neighbors nearer than eight miles," so home and loom shed—and the loom—were abandoned.[13]

A number of points emerge from Mary Rabb's account, written for her children to share "the trials and troubles . . . here in Texas."[14] First, home textile production could be a rhythmic, centering activity that released one tempo-rarily from the worries and isolation of frontier life. Sec-ond, it was a source of pride, an important measure of a woman's industry and ability to provide for her family. Third, it wasn't easy, although Mary doesn't play up the difficulties. By one estimate, it took "two weeks of steady and earnest labor to spin enough thread" for a woman's dress, followed by a week at the loom and perhaps another week to do the cutting and hand-sewing.[15] The spinning wheel and loom most likely did not represent craftsmanship so much as crude practicality—John made the loom in two days—and the conditions under which Mary spun and wove, while exuding a certain romantic appeal, had to be less than ideal, given other demands on her time and such factors as mosquitoes, extreme heat, and sudden cold spells. Further, the Rabbs's mobility, by no means unusual for the time and region, rendered null any advances in ease of production to the point of leaving Mary without a loom once again.

Moreover, textile historian Jane Parker has pointed out that isolated women engaged in spinning and weaving, instead of becoming "centered," might find themselves focusing on their worries or longingly remembering when these activities were carried out among female family and friends. This is undoubtedly true in some cases, as is the fact that textile tasks often proved burdensome (see Chapter 3). But clearly Rabb and others drew satisfaction and solace from their solitary time at the wheel and loom.

Once colonists became fairly stable members of a community, however far-flung, some specialization of labor began, with certain women, because of necessity or skill, producing cloth for their neighbors. The informal arrangements demonstrated women's participation in the local economy, very much like the colonial bartering system that Laurel Thatcher Ulrich has described in frontier Maine in the late 1700s.[16]

For example, another early Austin colonist, Mrs. William Alley-McCoy, moved to Texas from Missouri with her husband and six children, the youngest a teenager, in 1822.

Six years later, Mrs. McCoy, now in her fifties, had lost her husband to a Karankawa Indian attack, one of her elder sons to a Comanche attack, and another to drowning. She began spinning and weaving for her neighbors, an early-twentieth-century chronicler calling the activity "service to her friends and family." But clearly economic survival was involved, as the same account notes that "through her labors and her plans through the spinning and weaving she began to see some foundation for a hope for a better day."[17]

Where home textile production continued to take place within the family for which it was intended, the whole family continued to be involved. Daniel Shipman was another early arrival in Austin's colony, he and his parents and siblings settling near San Felipe in the early 1820s. As he recalled, "Our mothers and sisters understood how to card, spin, weave, cut out and make our clothes, and that was not all, for some of their sons knew how to help them." The family gathered the cotton and piled it near the hearth-fire to make it warm, then processed it through a hand gin, placing the seedless lint in a basket. (In this step, they were more fortunate than those settler families who continued to pick the seeds out by hand for years.) Eventually, the cotton would emerge from the loom as "jeans, counter-panes, coverlets, etc."[18]

Shipman associated mothers with the woven cloth, and normally daughters were trained to do the spinning, the older women handling the more complicated task of dressing the loom and weaving. But Mrs. Goldsby Childers, who moved in 1835 to what is now the Coryell-Bell County area, "saw to it that each daughter did her share" by teaching her to card, spin, and weave. Dilue Rose Harris, who arrived in Austin's colony from Missouri at age eight, would recall nine-year-old twin neighbor girls who knew how to both spin and weave. Dilue herself learned how to spin after a local wheelwright made a wheel for her already skilled mother. Dilue spun thread for her father's plow-lines, as "there was not any rope in the country."[19]

While spinning was considered the more accessible of the two skills, it required patience and practice, whether on the "great wheel" or, increasingly, on the smaller "sitting wheel" suitable for finer cotton spinning. A later frontier girl, Sarah Harkey Hall of San Saba County, would recall that at first the task seemed "impossible," but when she relaxed and received gentle instruction, she soon "could draw out a thread."[20] Girls were often fascinated with their mothers' webs of cloth on the loom but when trying their own hand grew frustrated with the monotonous threading that preceded the cloth making, and with the fact that the most minor treadling error would show up in misplaced threads in the cloth. And even skilled spinners and weavers experienced the frustrations of trying to produce with make-shift equipment and with a plethora of other demands on their time.

Most of the women and girls moving into Texas during this era were members of yeoman farming families, but there also began an influx of slaves and mistresses, both facing the same textile challenges, but on a larger scale. Slaves, too, made plow-lines, and slaves and mistresses alike worked to provide clothing and linens for a large farm or plantation population. What information exists concerning their activity comes primarily from Anglo sources and is problematic, reflecting an ethnocentric viewpoint in which Anglo skills and achievements are highlighted.

For example, we are told that plantation mistresses taught their slaves to spin and weave, and undoubtedly some did. But obscured is the fact that, as John Vlach notes, "most slaves were craftspeople in some way."[21] Many slaves were already more expert than their mistresses in the use of

Mothers on the Texas frontier passed along to their daughters the spinning skills they had learned in Tennessee and Missouri, in Alabama and Arkansas.

the spinning wheel and loom, for in some cases slave women had been performing these tasks for generations or had simply learned with alacrity. A Texas slave from Mississippi would recall her early training with pride: "I was a master hand when it come to weaving an sewing close fer white an colored. Yassum, I could dye de cloth an strip[e] it all pretty on de loom."[22]

Although this study uncovered no records showing Texas slave women being offered or purchased for these skills, nineteenth-century southern newspaper advertisements alluded to slave women's sewing, knitting, and spinning abilities. It seems certain that these skills were factored into owners' decisions in buying and placing values on some of their female slaves, as weavers were among those "enjoying the highest status within [the plantation] system."[23]

Who did what, and what degree of control was exerted, differed from plantation to plantation. In general, women and girls, black and white, regularly engaged in knitting to meet the heavy demand for socks and stockings; the portability of this activity meant that slave women knitted as they moved about the plantation, even, as one African-American said of her southern slave mother, while "sit[ting] on top of the mule on her way to the field."[24]

According to Anglo accounts, some mistresses would not trust their charges with the weaving of fine cloth. Such an attitude reflects the prevailing southern view of slaves as childlike and limited in ability, a view used to justify the patriarchal plantation system. The distrust may have been valid, but not for the reason cited; slaves were often weary from other duties and had no hope of ever wearing anything so fine. As one slave woman from the Palo Pinto area put it, "We'uns makes all the cloth for to makes the clothes, but we don't get 'em."[25] Most of these women naturally had little incentive to devote much effort to the craft. While many nonetheless did prove good textile workers, others— tired, unsuited to the task, or resistant—did not.

Whether they didn't think the slaves capable or didn't trust them with the task, some mistresses did not have slaves do any weaving. In fact, the account of Frances Grigsby Smythe, another young colonist of the early 1820s, in Annie Doom Pickrell's *Pioneer Women in Texas* indicates that the Grigsby family slaves were not trusted even with the finished product of the loom. Frances "carded both wool and cotton. She spun the carded article into thread, and she wove the thread into cloth to be used in clothing herself and the family and the slaves. Six cuts [lengths of 144 yards] of thread she must card and spin day by day or its equivalent in value in some other part of the cloth-making process. She must help, too, with the cutting and sewing of garments for the slaves, for few negro women could ever be trusted with this precious cloth to cut it into garments, even for their own children."[26]

Similarly, Isabella Harris McCrocklin, who arrived in Texas from Kentucky as a young married woman in 1832, was said to have carded and spun, to have scoured the woods for dyestuffs, and then to have woven material for both her family and their slaves.[27]

Mistresses who took on the textile production this fully surely must have felt it an overwhelming burden, feeding a common perception among hard-worked mistresses that each was "the slave of slaves."[28] Those who would have welcomed turning over some aspects of production to slaves may also have been frustrated by having little or no say as to how the slaves' labor was to be directed.

Apparently more common was the mistress's overseeing slave textile production, either as an expert or simply as a supervisor with the necessary basic knowledge of the processes. Either way, hierarchical southern plantation culture valued a mistress's ability to make her slaves perform the necessary tasks. "She controlled her slave women, taught them to spin, to weave," an early twentieth-century admirer wrote of Irish native and Texas immigrant Margaret Daniels Linn.[29] Perhaps more typical in showing both control and collaboration is an account of Sarah Morrison Hornsby, who moved to Texas from Mississippi with her husband in 1830 and settled at Hornsby's Bend, now in Bastrop County. "As soon as the cabin home was acceptably clean, and the scant furniture in place, Sarah put her [slave] women to work at loom and spinning wheel [using cotton and wool probably carried with them]. . . . Sarah with her children and her slaves then searched the woods for certain herbs and shrubs and barks to make dyestuffs in the hope of improving the appearance of the rough, heavy cloth, which this wise woman knew must before long be depended upon entirely as clothing for her family and her slaves."[30]

This mutual dependence on what could be produced within the frontier household, and mutual effort in producing it, no doubt often fostered a closer and more congenial relationship between slave and mistress than could thrive in more established areas. Ann Malone explains, "Especially in the most remote and exposed areas, a strong emotional bond occasionally developed between the white and black members of frontier households as they both sought to cope with the challenges and insecurities of their new existence. . . . If not an equal relationship, it was at least more reciprocal than was common under normal plantation conditions."[31]

Frontier mistresses and slaves might even commiserate over each other's ugly daily wear. Anglo women often resisted making use of the few finer clothes and fabrics they possessed. Maris Davis Jones-Carter, a Mississippi native who married in Texas in the early 1830s, carefully preserved a black silk dress brought from Mississippi. She guarded "precious linen" brought from her old home and cloth "bought from an unexpected peddler" even from her own daughters as the whole family and the slaves continued to produce "ugly cotton and woolen cloth," apparently for everyday wear for all.[32]

Among slave-holding families, daughters, too, were instructed and involved in textile production, both in their

Skilled slave women and mistresses consulted each other in meeting the clothing and linen needs of the plantation household.

roles as children of the frontier and as future mistresses. Sarah Stafford Dyer of San Felipe, Austin's colony, taught her daughters "to piece quilts, to spin and to weave and to make their own clothes and clothes for the slaves."[33]

When fiber, equipment, time, and skill allowed for something beyond the most rudimentary homespun, sometimes female members of the plantation family reserved the right to produce finer fabrics, no doubt finding such production comfortably fitting their gendered role as creators of aesthetically pleasing textiles. Frances Grigsby was reported to have been weaving an elaborate counterpane in her Texas home when she first met husband George Smythe.[34]

Still, slave women were usually the primary textile producers on Texas plantations—one pioneer plantation home was said to look like a factory, with slaves working away at wheels and looms—and the mistresses often charged them with producing not only slave cloth, mattress covers, and cotton-picking sacks but also high-quality fabrics. Slaves of Alvinia White Nail, who moved to Texas in 1830, turned out material for the family's clothing and "sheets, towels, even bed-spreads heavily woven, the flowers in the pattern heavily tufted."[35] Jean Black Williams, who settled with her husband at Washington-on-the-Brazos about 1833, would have her slaves produce not only blankets but also the cloth for her son's wedding suit.

If Anglo girls and women often found frustrating and difficult such time-consuming activity, slave women certainly found it more so. While some enjoyed better treatment and some artistic control because of their skills, most were compelled to perform hard labor all day, were poorly fed, clothed, and housed, and were faced at night with textile quotas to meet. The lives of slave textile producers will be dealt with in the next chapter, as it covers the period in which the southern plantation system developed more fully in Texas, but certainly Texas slave women, like the Virginia slave workers mentioned earlier, had to "keep their eyes on the sun" as they labored to produce the coarse fabric that was their lot, or labored to meet their mistresses' standards to produce finer cloth for the planter family's use.

Whether slave or free, the number of migrants filtering into Texas from the East remained small during the 1820s. Only Austin and DeWitt managed to settle many people—in 1830, over four thousand in Austin's colony and 150 families in DeWitt's. The Mexican government edict of 1830 banning further American immigration and the importation of slaves temporarily reduced the influx. Yet the flow could not be halted, and European families were beginning to immigrate to Texas as well. European women's textile production abilities naturally depended on their own cultural backgrounds, and there are indications that region of origin and socioeconomic status had a great deal to do with their proficiency. While some came with spinning and weaving skills, Caroline Ernst von Roeder von Hinueber, whose German family immigrated to Austin's colony via New York and New Orleans in 1831, would write, "Our supply of clothes was . . . insufficient, and we had no spinning wheel, nor did we know how to spin and weave like the Americans."[36]

Von Hinueber also commented on the crude living conditions of the Texas frontier; her family's first home of its own was "a miserable little hut" with a porous straw roof and moss sides on which the cows nibbled.[37] Her father abandoned his attempts to build a log and clay chimney when the family considered the danger of the house catching fire.

While other pioneers could improve on such a dwelling, the houses of this period were at best rough log cabins with very limited space. A loom took up much of that precious space, so when possible, it was placed for use in another structure—a special shed (such as John Rabb built), or perhaps a preexisting outbuilding. When this was not possible, families might dismantle and store the loom temporarily. But the need and the extent of labor required made home textile production a year-round activity; while families might concentrate on the spinning for a period, knowing that the loom would quickly consume the product of many a day's work at the wheel, they often could not do without the loom for long. Further, time for weaving would more likely be found in agrarian households in the late fall and winter months, after the harvest and during the season when bad weather forced families indoors. This meant that textile production took up the most space just when the family felt the most cramped.

Another frontier condition that affected home textile production was the frequent lack of adequate light. Pioneer homes boasted few windows, and people "moved themselves, or perhaps more specifically their furniture, around a room to follow the sunlight coming through the windows."[38] At first, the fireplace provided the home's only evening light. Daniel Shipman would remember that his family burned dry cane to create light in the evenings.

Immigrants made or purchased tallow candles, but these gave off less light than the desirable and expensive sperm candles made with oil from the head cavity of the sperm whale. Tallow candles also had to be "snuffed," the burnt wick end repeatedly removed "to keep the candle from guttering and smoking."[39] During this period, braided candle-wicking, which eliminated the need for snuffing, was introduced and eagerly sought at the general store or spun and twisted at home. Some families were able to use wax from bee trees in their candle making.

Lamps initially were nothing more than a twisted rag wick secured in a shallow container of lard; one Austin colonist recalled that, lacking lard, he "hunted [racoons] and rendered oil from their fat" for this purpose.[40] Whale oil was soon available to some, and camphene lamps—unfortunately highly flammable—enjoyed some popularity in the 1830s. But until kerosene would become a standard lighting source in the 1850s, most rural Texans depended primarily on candles for lighting. Further, they tried to extend the life of tallow candles by sprinkling salt on them, the result being a sickly, flickering flame.

For home textile workers, this meant that the most exacting work had to be performed in the poorest of lights. Those who could do so planned their weaving and fine sewing for the daylight hours, their spinning, knitting, and plain sewing for the evening. But the work had to be done whenever it could be accomplished, and many a pioneer child remembered going to sleep to the steady thump of weft thread being beat into the warp or to the whirr of the great wheel as a mother walked back and forth, back and forth, drawing the fiber into thread late into the night.

There was limited experimentation with other fibers during this period. Some families raised and processed flax for linen. In his 1836 immigrant guide, David Edward recounts "coming upon a small field of it, in a cleared cane bottom, growing as beautiful as any I had ever seen in Europe." And in 1835 there occurred in East Texas "an unsuccessful attempt to propagate the silkworm." But with sheep raising common—one Grimes County plantation in the 1820s was already producing "a very good quality of woolen goods"—and with cotton beginning its ascendance as Texas' primary crop, wool and cotton were simply the most available and most used fibers.[41] And like their frontier predecessors, Texas women in this period concentrated almost exclusively on practical, durable cloth—linsey-woolsey and jean.

They did, however, try to enliven the homespun with color. Nature provided a bonus in Texas with the presence of wild indigo, which required extended processing but did not need a mordant and yielded true blues. Edward's guide noted it growing "in luxurious profusion" and blithely obscured the work involved in converting it to dye by noting it "requir[ed] only the aid of an industrious house-wife to produce a dye, if not superior, yet equal to the far famed Prussian blue." In her 1833 description of Texas, Mary Austin Holley, too, noted indigo "grow[ing] wild on the sides of the road like the milkweed of Kentucky" and found the dye "manufactured by families for domestic use, and. . . preferred to imported indigo."[42]

Another highly valuable natural dye, "the only wild source of a strong, colorfast red dye in Texas," was that of the cochineal, a minute insect that lives on the pads of the prickly pear cactus in southern, central, and western Texas. Travelers during this period noted the dye potential of the insect and its cultivation by indigenous Texas tribes, but no pioneer accounts found mention collecting and processing the bugs for dye.[43]

Commercial mordants and dyes—indigo and cochineal, logwood and madder—made their way early onto pioneer mercantile shelves, but they remained literally and financially beyond the reach of many a woman settler. So in addition to harvesting or growing indigo, women continued to look to the woods for roots, barks, nuts, moss, flowers, and weeds. Betty Mills in her *Calico Chronicle* describes some of the possibilities: "Bark from the walnut, cedar, and butternut trees made a satisfactory brown. Actually, butternut could produce a range from gray to dark brown. Logwood made black; boiled sumac berries gave a warm red, as did madder. Peach and hickory bark, boiled onion skin, and copperas all furnished different shades of yellow. Purple came from oak and maple bark, and gray from cedar berries."[44]

Again, the results at their best were seldom vivid, especially by late-twentieth-century standards, but rather soft and muted earth tones.[45]

Women searched woods and fields for plants that would yield attractive colors.

As women spread among the isolated farms and plantations of the Texas colonies continued this work of centuries, their political environment was changing rapidly. Tensions building between the Mexican government and the American immigrants would erupt into the Texas Revolution in late 1835, as the American population neared thirty thousand. Of course, the hostilities exacerbated frontier uncertainties. Commenting on the varied, rag-tag attire of the revolutionary forces that marched to take over San Antonio in late 1835, Noah Smithwick noted a "shaggy brown buffalo robe contrast[ing] with a gaily checkered counterpane" that demonstrated "all the skill of

dye and weave" of its maker, perhaps a young wife who wove "daydreams" into it, little anticipating "that it might be [her husband's] winding sheet."[46]

In the wake of news of the Alamo's fall in spring, 1836, families abandoned homesteads and joined what became known as the Runaway Scrape of 1836, a pell-mell retreat to the east to escape Santa Anna's armies.

When one could grab only a few items, what would one choose? Maria Bachman Atkinson of Austin's colony loaded into a box "some balls of spun cotton" which she planned "to braid into bridles for the horses."[47] Reaching Groce's Crossing and tiring of her burden, she left the box with prominent colonist Jared Groce and proceeded eastward.

Sam Houston's startling victory over Santa Anna at

San Jacinto ended the Revolution and halted the exodus. Maria returned to Groce's Crossing to reclaim her box, but it had been broken into, the cotton stolen. The emptied box was a portent of sorts, for frontier uncertainties and the necessity of starting over would characterize Texas life and stimulate home textile production as the new republic struggled for survival, then as the fledgling state expanded.

The Republic &
Early Statehood
Years, 1836–1860

*"Yes we had some good times, too. We worked. We spun
thread both cotton and wool, and we wove it into cloth.
Sometimes the Indians would bother . . . but then we'd
forget even Indians when we got together."*
—Mary Hill Williams,
of her days growing up in Bastrop County

IT IS TEMPTING TO DUB THE QUARTER-
century that began in 1836 the age of homespun in Texas.
Such a title might seem misleading, as home textile production was by no means universal; on the heels of the
Revolution, merchants in the settlements with access to
coastal ports were advertising a profusion of fabrics, from
muslin to silk, and some ready-made clothes. Further, with
the domestic artisan tradition fading in the East and even
the South, and with sewing becoming the specialized focus

of women's textile activity, the new generations of women immigrating to Texas were less likely than were the early colonists to possess spinning and weaving skills. Still, a large number of women and girls during this period remained remarkably busy producing yarn and cloth at home.

In these years, the Texas frontier expanded steadily northward and as far west as geographic conditions and the Comanches would allow. From Austin's colony on the coastal prairies and in the forested river bottoms, from the settlements spilling over the Louisiana line into the piney woods of far southeast Texas, immigrants pushed north-ward and westward to the blackland prairie and post oak belt of central Texas and to the blackland prairie and woods of northeast Texas. Between 1850 and 1860, they edged out into the south Texas brush country, the north central Texas grand prairie, and the adjoining woodland belts called the Cross Timbers, willing to face the land's relative aridity and the Comanche threat.[1]

The political developments of the era both retarded and stimulated this movement. Between 1836 and 1845, Texas had republic status but remained an uncertain fron-tier in every sense, plagued by lack of an adequate treasury, by recurrent hostilities with the Mexican military and with West Texas Indians, and by controversies over boundary lines. Admission to the Union in 1845 brought an easing of tensions with Mexico and a federal government to pro-vide funds, services, and protection against Indians. But even so, most of Texas remained a remote and inadequately governed frontier, with rail lines and other transportation improvements failing to develop, with virtually no indus-try, and with the Comanches unsubdued.

Still, the people came, especially between 1850 and 1860, when the population almost tripled to over six hun-dred thousand. Contingents of European emigrants, especially Germans, began arriving in great numbers in the early 1840s. They came both better and more poorly prepared than their Texas neighbors. As Anne Malone explains, "In some ways the immigrant woman did have a psychological advantage over her English and Anglo American counterpart for she was better accustomed to a strong economic role," her background in a "peasant or agricultural" society conditioning her for "the hard labor and role adjustments [she] would encounter in Texas."[2]

But the women of the European emigration varied in background and skills, and all of them faced a host of heightened challenges. For example, even those women who arrived from a tradition of agricultural labor were used to a well-established village life and easy availability of goods.[3] The Texas propaganda in their homelands had contained little practical information and advice, and what there was had been directed to the men and their concerns. Nor could the women benefit from much direct contact with more experienced frontier dwellers, as the European enclaves remained relatively isolated.

Among the largest immigrant group, the Germans, regional and socioeconomic origins varied greatly over time. If a German woman did have spinning and weaving knowledge, she often was stymied in planning to use it by being allowed only one trunk for all the possessions with which she would start anew in Texas. Arriving on the frontier, she had adaptations to make, as her experience was with wool or flax rather than the primary fiber of the realm, cotton.[4]

Meanwhile, the bulk of the migration continued to come from the American South, particularly from the states of Tennessee and Alabama, both with well-established home textile traditions.

As they spread along the rivers, across the prairies, into the timbered regions, some women began textile production with materials brought from former homes. Sarah Lane Scott, who immigrated to Grimes County from Mississippi in 1838, was said to have transported with her spinning wheels, cotton fiber, even looms and to have put her slave women to work immediately on new wagon covers in anticipation of a further move.[5]

Others carried as many textile items as possible, including finer linens that bespoke the relative comfort and leisure of a former home. But women had difficulty preserving these linens under rough frontier conditions, and sometimes—as with the Utah immigrant party on the Platte River—sheets suddenly became shrouds. Sarah Morrison Hornsby, living in Bastrop County during the republic period, found two young Texas army men, sent to guard her family from Indians and Mexicans, hacked to death by Indians in her cornfield. She buried them in sheets brought with her from Mississippi.[6]

One way or another, most immigrants experienced the same dearth of clothing and linens as their predecessors had faced a decade or two before. A certain frontier pride and sartorial splendor continued to be associated with buckskin; J. Taylor Allen noted that, when his father came from Tennessee to Texas in 1836, "the clothing consisted of dressed deer skin, hunting shirt, pants, vest, leggins, moccasins, and coon skin cap." But need remained the primary criterion for choosing buckskin dress. T. U. Taylor would recall of his boyhood days in early Parker County, established in the 1850s, "Clothing must be to a great extent obtained from [animals] as we were so remote from the markets therefore the hides of the wild animals were used." Sarah Harkey Hall would remember of her family's struggle for survival in San Saba County that her father would kill and dress deerskins and her mother "would make coats and pants of those dress[ed] hides for my brothers and would sometimes make whole suits for men and sell them."[7]

Meanwhile, Hall's mother was spinning and weaving not only clothes for herself and her daughters but also blankets and other household linens. Although commercial wheels and looms were being produced in the United States in the 1840s, male family or community members still produced most of the necessary equipment. Hall's father "was continually busy in his shop making wheels, reels, warping bars and looms for manufacturing cloth." T. U. Taylor recalled of his Parker County boyhood that looms were home produced, "all [their] accessories . . . made in the neighborhood." Dora Nabers Greene, who moved to Comanche County with her family at age three, would remember, "When I was ten years old father bought me a wheel that old man Griffy made, sawed it off for me to use."[8] About 1860, German emigrant Elise Henrich of Fredericksburg received as a wedding present from her uncle Mathias Boos a spinning wheel he had made "from walnut wood cut from trees on the Pedernales River"—and she used it.[9]

For fiber, some settlers chose to grow flax in the time-honored colonial and European traditions. Helen Mary Kirkpatrick Tinnin, who moved to Travis County from Arkansas with her husband in 1850, directed her slaves in planting flax along the Colorado River and oversaw the process by which the flax was converted into linen sheets. In the 1850s, the raising of Angora goats in central Texas led to some mohair textiles being produced.[10] But cotton was the most obvious choice for home textile production, since it was cultivated so widely and became quickly the premier cash crop; wool and cotton-wool combinations, too, remained popular.

As in the earlier decades on Texas frontiers, whole families and communities contributed to the cloth-making process. Men not only sheared sheep and constructed and re-paired equipment but also entered into the textile work at various stages. One man in Dora Greene's Comanche County community, Old Grandpa Barcroft, was much sought after by the women as a carder because "he could card real fast and spin good rolls and the woman he carded for spun the most thread." Dora's father sized, or stiffened and strength-ened the warp yarn her mother spun so that the weaving would go smoothly: "He made a thin gruel of meal in the wash pot. After the thread was . . . ready to go on the warping bars, he dipped it in the gruel and hung on frames to dry. Then from a winding blade, the thread was wound on long corn cobs which were fastened on long spikes driven in a long board. Then each end was tied tight together so it would not slip and was ready to fasten to the warping bars. He would take all the thread from the cobs, take it down and place it on the big beam of the loom."[11] Boys helped pick the chaff from wool and occasionally helped gather dyestuffs. They might be charged with picking the cotton seeds out by hand or processing the fiber through a hand gin, but community cotton gins soon relieved all but the most far-flung frontier families of this task.

There are occasional references to boys learning to spin and weave during this period. Polish immigrant Constantina Adamietz, who settled as a child in present-day Bandera County in 1855, reported, "Every girl learned to spin and weave and many of the boys learned it too," while former slave Stearlin Arnwine of Washington County noted of his growing-up years, "I learned to spin and weave and knit and made lots of socks."[12]

No accounts were uncovered of men on the frontier actually spinning and weaving during this period, but the census of 1850, which did not specify occupations for women, showed "eleven professional [male] weavers at work

Family members shared in the chore of picking the seed from cotton so that it could be carded and spun.

in seven counties of the state." Primarily European emigrants, most were part of an extended family or boarded in a family. For example, in 1850, James Curry, a forty-three-year-old native of Ireland, was listed in Cass County, living with the Ritchie family. That same year, another Irishman, seventy-five-year-old John McCastoro, was included in a nine-member Brazos County household in which the surname Robinson predominated. In the 1860 census, "Texas reported only three working male weavers," including Evaristo Montillo in El Paso County and thirty-five-year-old W. E. Fouch from Prussia, a boarder in a Harris County household.[13]

European emigrants, especially the elderly McCastoro, may well have done some weaving for the families and communities with which they were connected, but more likely the term "weaver" was a definition of their skilled trade past rather than of their present and future, as they had entered an environment in which either commercial cloth was available or the bulk of the cloth production for family and community was handled by women and girls within their households. The tradition of the professional guild weaver had not survived in America, nor did the limited colonial and early republic tradition of the independent professional male weaver, capable of producing everyday fabric and elaborate overshot or Jacquard coverlets, appear to extend to Texas to any noticeable degree.

Ample evidence exists of women's continuing role in the home production of textiles and of their daughters' labor and training in this area. Sometimes it is only implied, as in Frederick Law Olmsted's report of an early 1850s visit to a German farmer who announced, "My stockings grew in the field yonder." Other accounts are less elliptical. J. Taylor Allen in reminiscing of his boyhood in Fannin County listed first among the activities of mothers and sisters "the hum of the spinning wheel, the bang, bang of the loom, the old time carding, warping, reeling and coloring of the good old time cloth." T. U. Taylor recollected that "after the mother & Daughters had washed the dishes at night they brought out the old Cards and combed the wool into rolls. . . ."[14]

The degree of industry required is reflected in a portrait of the activities of Frances Lipscomb Van Zandt, who settled in Harrison County in 1842: "She spun the cotton and the wool into thread, and then wove it into cloth. She made the cloth into clothes, the sewing all done by hand. She made her husband an overcoat from a wool blanket, carded the remaining scraps into thread, and knit the thread into comfortable socks. . . ."[15]

As this mention of carding scraps into thread shows, every bit of yarn, every fragment of cloth was often judged valuable, and whole new fabric obviously even more so. One Bell County man elected to the state legislature responded to a fellow legislator's desire to own a suit similar to his by proudly revealing, "None can be bought, for my wife spun the thread, wove the cloth and made the suit." Men who grew up on the Texas frontier often had pleasant, romantic memories of their mothers' and sisters' labor, the "hands of true and noble womanhood" always at work.[16]

Women clearly took pride in their production abilities, but even for those skilled in cloth making, the demands could be overwhelming and daughters' labor was necessary. Some girls eagerly learned the intricacies of their mothers' textile activities. Ten-year-old Dora Nabers Greene received her own spinning wheel from her father because "as soon as I would find a wheel idle, I would slip in and try to spin—sometimes I would muss up the [carded] rolls, and cause trouble. . . ."[17] Some learned quickly and enjoyed challenging themselves in terms of quantity or quality.

But others associated the tasks with privation and even terror. "My earliest recollection was the fear of Indians and trying to catch the sunshine through the cracks of our little log cabin and the horror I had to the hum of the spinning wheel," one frontier daughter would report. To her and many others, textile production looked and proved onerous.[18] Women who grew up on the Texas frontier were often more closely attuned to the difficulties their mothers experienced than were male family members. While children might take drowsy comfort in their mother's steady spinning of a wheel or beating of a loom through the night, girls at some point had to realize how tired was the woman employing this equipment, how much work of a demanding and repetitive nature was in store for them. And indeed, as overworked mothers trained them, sometimes with understandable impatience, many were soon having to spin a number of "cuts" per day, to knit a quota of three or more socks per week.

As they became more proficient, adolescent girls became closely identified with the role of spinner and even of weaver. The 1850 census asked only for "Profession, Occupation, or Trade of each Male Person over 15 years of age," but the 1860 census substituted "each person, male and female" for "each Male Person." Girls who produced yarn and cloth for their families and perhaps for barter or sale in their communities began to appear as workers in the rolls. For example, J. A. Pumpkin, a sixteen-year-old female in Bowie County, was listed in the 1860 census as a weaver. She apparently lived with her parents, listed as "farmer" and "lady," with an eighteen-year-old brother, listed as "farm laborer," and with a number of younger siblings.[19]

The Henderson County census taker, more thorough than his fellows, recorded something under "Occupation" for each family member. Thus, we have a record of "45 weavers in the county, mostly young women between the ages of 15 and 20," often with younger sisters listed as spinners.[20] Typical were Lydia H. Boles, "weaver," age 19, and Elizabeth A. Boles, "spinster," age 18. In the Reynolds family, daughter Catharine, age 20, was a weaver, while her mother and older sister were listed simply as "domestics."[21]

The 1860 census listed mature women, too, as textile producers. The census identified a number as blanket makers in Zapata County, which listed a total of thirty women weavers. (Many of the women had emigrated from the Middle South, leading Diane Greene Taylor to speculate that Zapata County was one place where European, American, and Mexican traditions "met and intermingled."[22]) In Cherokee County, thirty-five-year-old Rachel Weddell, a weaver from Illinois, shared a home with another weaver, forty-six-year-old Mary Molden from Arkansas, and with a sixty-five-year-old female "knitter." In Erath County, Adaline Bright and Rosamunda Boll both gave their age as forty, their home of origin as Tennessee, and their occupation as "weaver." In Henderson County, thirty-eight-year-old Mary Ann Powers, wife of a farmer and mother of a large family, was listed as a weaver rather than simply as a "domestic" or "House Keeper."[23]

Clearly, some women produced textiles for barter or cash. Susannah Tate Cunningham of Comanche County on rainy days "wove cloth for her neighbors on her home loom or on the loom of her patron, taking many times in payment for such labor just as much corn as she could herself carry home."[24] As in the previous era, textile production provided one of the limited, gendered options for financially strapped women to enter into the local economy.

Textile production was also a traditional activity for young women and their female family members as the former prepared for marriage. Mary Palmer and Tacitus Kennerly courted for three years before marrying in 1851; during that time, Mary and her sisters produced a dowry of "homespun sheets, pillow-cases, towels, blankets, too."[25]

Whether working to meet their own needs in setting up housekeeping, or to meet the family's needs or the community's, women produced a wide variety of goods. For the home, they spun and wove huck towels, muslin curtains, and even cloth ceilings after the style of the Hispanic population; the two main rooms in Harriet Bachman Jourdan's home on Walnut Creek in Bastrop County in the late 1840s were "ceiled with canopies of homespun." Women made sacks, sheets and covers, "home spun and corded and woven blankets, quilts and bed ticking."[26]

The more skilled and tenacious produced intricate coverlets, like their eastern sisters favoring overshot designs with vivid names—Doors and Windows, Texas Check, Tennessee Trouble, Bonaparte's March—the dyed wool overshot pattern weft alternating with plain-weave cotton weft in crossing a cotton warp.

The women also, of course, created material for clothing, converting it into men's and boys' trousers, coats, vests, and shirts, into women's and girls' everyday dresses, bloomers, and even wedding dresses.

The clothing tended to be "tough and durable," passed down from one brother or sister to another. It was also often thick and bland; homespun women's apparel were referred to as "heavy dresses." As one memoralist wrote, "Even the women who made that homespun cloth failed to lay any claim to beauty for the product of their tiresome labor."[27]

The weaving of patterns with dyed yarn helped enliven the product. Amzina Wade remembered of her youth in northeastern Texas homemade linsey-woolsey dresses and matching bloomers "woven in stripes and plaids of gay colors." Commercial dyestuffs, such as madder, indigo, and logwood, were being regularly advertised in Houston papers in the mid-1840s as well as mordants, such as copperas. But as in the past, families primarily made use of the natural dyestuffs surrounding them. Traveling in Texas in 1842, William Bollaert noted the common practice of dyeing with either the wild indigo or the introduced Spanish indigo: "The indigo plant is boiled . . . strained, then agi-

The Horsemint plant was among many collected for dyes it would yield.

tated or churned for some time; lime water or the juice of some very astringent vegetable is added to it, and it is left to precipitate or settle to the bottom, the liquor is drawn off, and the blue mass or indigo left to dry."[28]

In Dallas County, where by 1850 "nearly every family raised considerable cotton for domestic use," sumac berries with a copperas mordant were commonly used.[29] Dora Nabers Greene would remember of her early years in Comanche County that wild plum roots yielded purple dye, that black jack bark with a copperas mordant produced black, and that walnut roots with copperas made a brown dye for her father's and brothers' wool winter jeans. Male family members crushed red rock from Rush Creek and came up with a brick red shade, while "Sister Mary took the yellow blooms of the broom weed and made a pretty yellow dye." With such results, Mary could make her mother "a sack of yellow and black plaid wool," herself "a dress of red and purple stripes."[30]

As in earlier days, most of this activity was conducted individually or within the family circle, but communal traditions persisted as well. Greene provides the most direct evidence of this in her reference to an annual "spinning" in "Old Cora" that resembles the town commons gatherings of colonial days: "Each woman would give a spinning in the fall. Mother would give one and serve a big dinner at home. Grandma Neely, Mrs. Marshall, Mrs. Barcroft, Mrs. James, Mrs. Kiser, Mrs. Puckett, Mrs. Takersley and all the other women in town, about 15 or 16 of them, carried their wheels to the church as it was the only place large enough to hold that many wheels."[31]

Even when women did not gather in a central location, the communal aspect of textile production was evident in the home as whole families processed the fibers, as female kin shared the skilled work, and as neighbors lent their assistance and expertise.

Many families owned or hired a few slaves who shared in the labor as well; J. Taylor Allen of early Fannin County recalled the spinning, weaving, and construction of clothing and bedding by noting, "The mother of the family, assisted by the negro servants, did this work. . . ." On small farms with only a few slaves, the mistress and slaves were likely to work together, the mistress doing the weaving. Abe Bean, one of six slaves on a South Texas farm, recalled that everyone there wore homemade clothes and "Ol' mistus she weave d' clof' herse'f."[32]

The record is extremely skimpy on the free black women residing in Texas during the antebellum period, but some did work as seamstresses; spinning and weaving would have been other avenues of employment open to them.

On the large plantations, communal textile activity was

the norm for many slave women. Southern plantation culture became firmly entrenched in Texas during its years of independence and early statehood. In 1837, slaves were concentrated only in parts of Austin's old colony and in certain areas along the Louisiana-Texas border. By 1858, they could be found throughout settled Texas and thickly distributed on the plantations of southcentral and northeast Texas.[33] Even then, only a small percentage of Texans owned many slaves, but this percentage to a great extent held the social, political, and economic power in the antebellum state.

On a well-established Texas plantation, slaves received a blanket every year or two and clothing allowances once or twice a year. The clothing allowance might be in the form of fabric meted out to individual families; planter Julian Sidney Devereux noted in his record book for his Rusk County plantation in February, 1853, that "Negro cloth [was] Given out in Families," with seventeen recipients claiming a total of 300 ½ yards.[34] This was probably cheap but durable commercial cloth, although after the Huntsville state penitentiary steam-powered mill opened in 1856, some planters purchased "negro cloth" from it, and at least one planter "customarily sent a bale of wool to Georgia, his former home, and had jeans of half wool and half cotton made for winter clothing for his servants."[35]

Many planter families—whether on frontier acreage or in settled areas—still found it economical to have their slave women process the cotton and wool produced on the plantation into clothing and blankets for the slave community. Former slave Della Mun Bibles recalled of her early life on a central Texas plantation that young slave women wore blue homespun made on the plantation and children—including the white children—went clad in brown homespun, but "the white folks had fine clothes of cloth bought at Austin and Houston." Traveling on the coastal prairies in 1842, William Bollaert noted "some 80 Negroes" at a Nixon's Creek plantation "spin and weave all their cotton and woolen clothing on this plantation and make the bagging and rope of cotton, for baling up the cotton for market."[36]

On some plantations, owners combined purchases of commercial cloth with slave-produced homespun to meet slave needs. On still others, all wore homespun. Adeline Cunningham, born a slave in Lavaca County, recalled the slave women making "all the clothes for old man Foley and his family and for the slaves."[37]

Many slave women performed this labor after they completed their normal field and "big house" labors of the day. Silvia King was a cook on a frontier plantation, probably in Fayette County, but she did double duty at the loom and spinning wheel and spoke of it with a certain pride: "On the cold winter nights, I sat many a time spinning with two threads, one in each hand and my feet on the wheel and the baby sleeping on my lap."[38]

Other members of slave families became involved in the extra labor. Former slave John Ellis would recall of his childhood, "After our day's work was done we would sit up at night and pick the seed out of the cotton so they could spin it into thread. Then we went out and got different kinds of bark and boiled it to get dye for the thread before it was spun into cloth."[39]

In addition to their evening work, slaves on some plantations would be put to textile production activities during inclement weather. Former slave Irella Walker of Bastrop County remembered that "a lot of women would stay in the cabins and spin thread for the looms" during these periods.[40]

All was not drudgery. Like their Anglo frontier counterparts, slave women often enjoyed the communal nature of their textile activity, one former southern slave recalling pleasant evenings spent as a group spinning, weaving, sewing, talking, and sharing jokes.[41] The presence of a cotton gin on some plantations, the gin used to process cotton both for sale and for domestic use, eased the labor. And planters making a long-term commitment to cloth production planned accordingly. They needed a good carpenter or carpenters; ex-slave Carey Davenport would remark of his carpenter father that he was "a very valuable man" because of his ability to "make spinning wheels and parts of looms."[42]

These owners also usually set aside textile work areas and adopted a division of labor, with certain girls and women freed from field work in order to concentrate on meeting the plantation's clothing and linen needs. Silvia King remembered, "There was spinning and weaving cabins, long with a chimney in each end." Former slave Cunningham noted that the textile production took place in the plantation owner's home, the workers women whose children were old enough to take their place in the fields.[43] Another former slave, Martha Ruffin, reported, "Massa had fifteen or twenty women carding and weaving and spinning most all the time."[44]

Slave women who worked as weavers not only generally enjoyed higher status than most of the plantation slaves but also "were often allowed to have their children in or near the work area." Skilled weavers continued to exercise some creative autonomy, although there is as yet no evidence of a distinctive nineteenth-century African-American weaving tradition.[45]

Slave girls, like their European counterparts, had trouble learning the skills and meeting quotas, but with much harsher consequences. "I saw one of my sisters whipped

Because looms took up so much space, they often occupied a separate "loom house."

because she didn't spin enough," Campbell Davis would recall. "They pulled her clothes down to her waist and laid her down on the stomach and lashed her with the rawhide quirt." Fannie Brown of Bell County would remember receiving "meny uh whuppen" from her mistress before she could master spinning and weaving duties, but the mistress was soon praising her work.[46]

The element of coercive violence is missing from the memoir of Fanny Yarborough, who took to textile production and spoke of it with pride. "We had to spin a brooch of thread every night. I learned all 'bout spinnin' and weavin' when I was little and by time I's 10 I'd made pretty striped cloth."[47]

But even if a slave girl spun and wove wonderfully, chances were that she remained woefully ill clothed. Just as owners often skimped on food and shelter for their charges, they also neglected adequate clothing. Randolph B. Campbell in *An Empire for Slavery: The Peculiar Institution in Texas* identifies standard twice-yearly clothing allowances as two dresses and two chemises for women and two shirts and two pairs of trousers for men, with field workers receiving coats or jackets in the winter. But daily wear and tear of such a limited wardrobe took its toll, and some owners failed to provide even this allotment. Former Bastrop County slave Richard Carruthers would recall almost freezing to death until he was placed before a fire and "poulticed . . . with sliced turnips." As he explained, "Come a norther and it blow snow and sleet, a poor old nigger don't have enough clothes to keep him warm and no way to get any more."[48]

Gen. James Hamilton, on a visit to the Retrieve plantation in Brazoria County, expressed dismay at the meager clothing of the slave workers but then found it no worse than "the average of Plantations in the County." William Bollaert in his 1842 travels repeated a telling Anglo justification of the situation: "It is said in Texas and in the U.S. by many as a serious *fact* that if a Negro child be kept clean and well clothed it will pine and often die; but if allowed to roll and play about in the dirt there is no fear of its thriving."[49]

White children, too, were consigned only the simplest, roughest shifts and long shirts during hard economic times, but these items remained standard attire for slave children long after many plantations had prospered, and slave men could only hope for a decent pair of trousers, women for a dress with any modicum of style.

Despite their drawbacks, material and clothing produced on plantations for slave wear did usually prove durable. One slave recalled, "Them wuz shirts that *wuz* shirts. If someone gets cot by his shirt on a limb of a tree he had to die there if he wern't cut down. Them shirts wouldn't rip no more than buckskin."[50]

Some owners did allow slaves to color the cloth for their use, and slaves acted as innovatively as their Anglo contemporaries, using indigo, "pokeberries, wild-peach bark, sweet-gum bark, and sumac," even clay.[51] They also tried "to individualize and 'dress up' their shapeless, plain, and drab plantation garb with edging, trimming, and even patching."[52] Often, slave women and girls would be allowed to produce a relatively nice dress or man's suit for their own wedding or that of a relative, perhaps with some assistance from the mistress.

Many slave women were skilled spinners, weavers, and seamstresses, but as noted in Chapter 2, the record concerning the variety and extent of their expertise is sketchy and obscured in traditional Anglo accounts by a celebratory emphasis on the industry, virtue, and skill of the plantation mistress. Thus, we are told repeatedly in Annie Doom Pickrell's *Pioneer Women of Texas* that a good mistress "made it her personal business to see that the colored women were taught . . . to cook, to sew, to spin" or "saw to it that her women slaves, the more intelligent among them, were taught to spin and weave." The mistress oversaw and participated in production; of Lucy Bugg Kyle, it was noted, "Under her direction and with her own help, her serving women carded the cotton, spun it into thread, wove it into cloth, and then her own dainty fingers fashioned the cloth into garments for her household, including her slaves."[53]

If the mistress's own dainty fingers did not do the actual work, she still received the credit. In Evelyn Carrington's *Women in Early Texas,* we are told that Helen Mary Kirkpatrick Tinnin, who with her husband established a plantation in Travis County, had her slaves weave and sew sheets from the plantation's own flax, and "How well she instructed [them] is shown by the tiny hems and stitches so beautifully done."[54]

Certainly, mistresses had tremendous responsibilities, and many no doubt had considerable textile skills that they passed along to their workers. But more likely in many cases is the situation described by Gladys-Marie Fry: "Old Miss and slave learned from each other, alternating the roles of teacher and student."[55]

Plantation mistresses of this era may have often lacked in-depth home-production skills, having come of age in the South at a time when commercial fabrics were readily available or when they could count on trained slave labor. Just as some accounts celebrate the skill and industry of the plantation mistress, a certain class-conscious celebration of her relative ignorance or passiveness is apparent in the following description of Mary Ann O'Connell Wallace Burleson, a Bastrop County resident of the mid-nineteenth century: "We have no records of any day or time when our Mary Ann had to use the spinning wheel or the loom or the needle. Slaves in plenty seemed to meet all these demands. . . ."[56]

At the same time, it should be noted that when mistresses did direct and engage in textile production, observers sometimes failed to comprehend the responsibility and effort involved. When William Bollaert in his travels stopped at a plantation between Columbus and Montgomery, he observed that the planter's wife, "though young and apparently delicately brought up, bustled about, amused herself weaving and kept the Negresses at their spinning."[57] Whoever did it—mistress, slave, or both working together— textile production took great time and effort and at least some skill. It is to be hoped that the young wife enjoyed her labor, but "amused herself weaving" ignores the essential nature of her activity and the perseverance and ability it required.

Throughout this period, most mistresses, along with slave women and women of Texas frontier families in general, continued to face myriad other household duties, in one way or another approximating Mary Crownover Rabb's daily schedule of spinning and milking and pounding meal and cooking and churning and minding children. And they continued to work under far-from-ideal conditions. They shivered or sweated over textile equipment in cabins and loom houses, performing tedious threading by the light of a pine knot or beef tallow candle. The more fortunate in the 1840s might possess a solar lamp, which made effective use of cheap oils, but it was not until the 1850s that a steady source of lighting arrived in the form of kerosene lamps.[58]

A chore related to the production of textiles was the care of clothing and linens. Much of women's labor went into mending and patching these items and darning socks, but these activities were minor compared to the onerous weekly duties of washing and ironing. On wash day, "blue Monday," women repeatedly lugged heavy buckets of water for washing, boiling, and rinsing, "from pump or well . . . to stove and tub." Susan Strasser describes what followed: "Rubbing, wringing, and lifting water-laden clothes and linens, including large articles like sheets, tablecloths, and men's heavy work clothes, wearied women's arms and wrists and exposed them to caustic substances. They lugged weighty tubs and baskets full of wet laundry outside, picked up each article, hung it on the line, and returned to take it all down; they ironed by heating several irons on the stove and alternating them as they cooled, never straying far from the hot stove." As Fry has pointed out, this work was not only hard on the workers, but on the textiles themselves.

Former slaves tell of boiling the wash with homemade lye in hollow logs, then beating it with a stick or having the barefooted children "tromp" it to remove dirt.[59]

As women continued to spin and weave, to mend and wash, the perpetual Indian threat, exacerbated by the thrust of settlements northwestward into Comanche territory, remained one of the most difficult challenges for many. Just as Sarah Morrison Hornsby had to use treasured sheets brought from Mississippi to bury the two young Texans killed by Indians early in this era, so approximately twenty years later Martha Speaks Vaughn used her own handwoven sheets to wrap the bodies of two visitors killed by Comanches after leaving her home.[60]

Women repeatedly "stood at the loom or the spinning-wheel" with rifles at hand, just as men kept weapons near them in the fields. Of one woman who bartered her weaving skills, it was noted, "She molded bullets when the weaving grew scarce, for the ever-present Indian and the beasts of the forest . . . made bullets just as much of a necessity as bread and meat."[61] The comment by Mary Hill Williams that opens this chapter suggests that, like Mary Rabb, many found solace from the threat in the absorbing nature of their textile work, although unlike isolated early settler Rabb, they were also able to gain solace from doing the work together.

Although pioneer conditions persisted even in some long-settled areas and continued to make home textile production necessary for a significant number of Texans, a few developments did signal a shift away from the home factory. For one thing, in addition to those men and women identified as weavers and spinners in the censuses of 1850 and 1860, a number of men were also listed as "wool carders," indicating that this function was becoming a commercial enterprise. For another, one finds more references

As immigrants moved deeper into Comanche territory, women kept rifles at hand as they spun and wove.

in this period to w o m e n ' s spinning strictly to produce knitting yarn; they could buy commercial cloth, thanks to burgeoning urban areas and steady supply lines, but they continued spinning in order to keep the family supplied with socks and other knitted items.[62]

A major change was signaled by the introduction of the sewing machine. Invented in 1846, it was "not generally in use in Texas until after the Civil War," but some Texas women before the war made the leap from use of a machine.[63]

The commercial cloth industry achieved some success in Texas. Just outside San Antonio in 1850, Salado Ranch Mills, "the earliest recorded cloth factory in Texas," used water power to produce "$15,000 worth of blankets and heavy woolen goods," its equipment consisting of "ninety spindles, two carding machines and three power looms." In 1856, Huntsville state penitentiary officials opened their mill; convicts quickly began producing "best quality osnaburg cotton and coarse woolen cloth." Three years later, equipment had more than doubled, and the prisoners were also turning out "lighter weight cotton, shirting, sheeting, kerseys, and cotton jeans," as well as thread and cotton batting. Despite the variety, the prison factory primarily provided unbleached, undyed "gray-goods" intended for "slave clothing, cotton bagging and other coarse uses."[64]

While the penitentiary operation has been judged the most successful of the early commercial factories, others soon followed. In Harrison County in the late 1850s, H. Ware established a factory in which his slaves produced "linsey, jeans, tweed, cassimere, Negro blankets, stocking yarns, and russet shoes" for sale.[65] By 1860, Panola County boasted a steam-run wool factory, Marshall a cotton and wool factory in which thirteen laborers turned out "tweeds, kerseys, linseys, and flannel."[66]

Texas in 1860, then, was moving away from the age of home cloth production. The previous quarter century had seen prodigious activity across the frontier and in plantation households, but as spinning and weaving waned in the eastern United States, new Texas immigrants were less likely to know the old home production methods and less likely to have to know them. Still, the old methods would survive among those self-reliant immigrants who continued to extend the frontier—and these methods would be dramatically revived throughout Texas as the Civil War thrust residents back into a struggle for basic necessities.

Chapter Four

The Civil War & the West Texas Frontier, 1860–1880

There was practically nothing left to buy. One turned again to spinning and weaving in order not to go about in rags.

—*Burnet County resident* Ottilie Goeth,
on the Civil War in Texas

ALTHOUGH FEW CIVIL WAR BATTLES WERE fought on Texas soil, the state's participation in the war affected citizens' lives in significant ways, forcing women in even the most well-established areas to return to the spinning wheel and loom or to attempt to spin and weave for the first time. Before exploring the changes war brought, however, we need to look again at the families of the far frontier, their daily lives little affected by wartime privation because the home factory and a subsistence lifestyle still remained for them the norm.

The memoirs of many pioneer children who grew up in the 1860s, those who lived along the western fringe of settlement in central and north-central Texas, refer matter-of-factly to home textile production. Gabriel Anderwald, a Polish emigrant of 1855, wrote of his boyhood days in Bandera County, "I wore homespun clothing, home made shoes and a hat plaited from wheat straw."[1]

In fact, some still felt lucky to own such attire. Bernard Fiedler was born in Fredericksburg in 1857; his family moved fifteen miles west of town about 1864. Of his boyhood, he would remember, "We had no clothes in those days. The best we had to wear was a shirt with a tail none too long. We had only one shirt at a time, too. When it became necessary to wash our shirts, the ladies would have to retire." Similarly, an early resident of Jack County would recall, "Boys up to fourteen years, some older, usually wore no trousers."[2]

In Fiedler's case, his mother obtained tanned deer hide and made buckskin trousers and vests for him and his brother. The boys immediately got the clothing wet with dew, then stayed out in the hot sun. The skin garments "shrank most shamefully" and became hard, rubbing their skin raw.[3]

The struggle to keep a frontier family clothed is perhaps nowhere else so fully addressed as in the memoirs of Sarah Harkey Hall. Sarah's parents—her father from North Carolina, her mother from West Virginia—had settled in San Saba County in the mid-1850s. Sarah was born in 1857, the fifth of thirteen children. The whole family worked constantly but scraped and struggled to meet their basic needs. Hall explained her mother's "fretfulness": "Her children were like stair steps and such a burden to card and weave, every thread we all wore, and make our clothes by hand. . . ." Sarah's two older sisters assisted, the oldest able to "spin filling at 8 years old," while Sarah herself acted as "baby nurse": "Oh! the hum of the wheel and the rattle of the cards made me weary, I knew my long weary day had begun—sitting by the cradle."[4] She also collected the dogwood sticks that served as the family's evening light source and with the younger children helped to pick the wool clean at night as her mother carded and her father taught the older ones.

Sarah tried to be resourceful, teaching herself to knit and straining to find ways to repair the two dresses that comprised her wardrobe one winter. "When my frock became so tattered and torn I would examine it closely to see if I could remedy it that it would appear more neatly. I soon saw by taking out the whole front and put[ting] in a new one it would be whole but where was I to get the cloth? All had been consumed and not a piece [left] over. . . . I had to do without."[5]

In 1864, the family collected and sold pecans, and Sarah's father purchased 250 yards of calico. The treasure this was for anyone in her frontier community is reflected in Sarah's comment, "Now I had a real fine frock, a calico dress and so many nice articles our neighbors didn't have." Her mother continued spinning and weaving cloth and blankets, "but was not in so great a restraint all the time." Sarah, too, learned to spin.[6]

Sarah's mother died suddenly in March, 1869 after a premature childbirth, and her father suffering from "dyspepsia, liver and kidney trouble, and rheumatism," followed within a few weeks. Before his death, he directed that the youngest child go to a relative but that the other siblings stay together on their homestead. At first, they did so, Sarah's two older sisters continuing to spin and the two oldest boys "carr[ying] on the general routine of business."[7]

But soon the sisters married, and the two brothers left home in an attempt to earn enough money for the brood.

Sarah, barely a teenager, was left alone with her little sister and brothers. "I sat and cried for the poor little things often and over again and wondered how are we to get clothes," she recalled.[8] At first, she simply labored to patch and piece from worn-out clothes, but she soon turned to her mother's old spinning wheel and began spinning thread and knitting socks for sale. Still, without another decent pecan crop, she and the children would have faced winter with a woefully inadequate supply of clothing and bedcovers; the last blanket woven by her mother had been taken by her oldest brother Joe when he had joined the Texas Rangers.

Joe was able to send some money, and the married sisters periodically took some of the children to live with them. But Sarah for a number of years had to worry, scrimp, and use every resource at her disposal to clothe and cover her younger siblings and herself. She spun, knitted, and sewed, buying fabric as she could. While her reminiscences of these years reveal the tremendous responsibility and despair she felt, some creativity and pride showed in her textile labors. Using commercial "ducken," or duck—a strong plain-weave cotton fabric—for her little brothers' trousers, she extracted a dye from "Shoneyhaw bushes" and colored the material a rich navy blue, causing a neighbor to exclaim with amazed pleasure, "What kind of goods is it Sarah? This is Ducken—Why, I never saw that color of Ducken."[9]

Another Texas frontier girl of the 1860s and early 1870s, Fannie Davis Beck, would write in much the same vein as a colonial child might have written a hundred years before,

"How many a night have I gone to sleep as I lay on the floor, watching my mother step back and forth, back and forth, holding her bat of cotton as she spun miles and miles of thread on large spindles."[10]

Beck's mother took the thread to a community weaver, Granny Lemons, who "wove cloth for dresses and underwear and men's shirts," as well as "a very rough wool cloth for men's suits."[11] Her customers did their own dyeing, if they wished any, and again, this was accomplished with materials from the environment—walnut bark, pokeberries, and roots.

While frontier women continued these age-old processes, all of Texas during the Civil War, like the South, experienced severe shortages of goods. Texans traditionally looked to the Gulf Coast for new goods to arrive via ship, but the Federals blockaded the coast in the summer of 1861, briefly captured the port town of Galveston in 1862, and took the crucial stretch of coastline between Matagorda and the mouth of the Rio Grande in late 1863. After both seizures, Confederate troops regained the area, but the federal blockade remained strong. Trade with Mexico continued, with Matamoras becoming a major cotton trade center for hordes of "speculators from the Union and the Confederacy, England, France, and Germany."[12] But Texans could look for only limited and erratic supplies from that quarter, and they could not expect material goods to filter in from southern states even more ravaged by the war. Despite the existence of those few fledgling textile factories in the years preceding the war, Texas and the other southern states still had a strong agrarian rather than industrialized economy.

Prices for cloth skyrocketed. Common jeans material cost three to five dollars a yard, common calico and muslin four to ten. Calico reportedly was being marketed at twenty-five dollars a yard, making something of a bargain the home-spun dress for which a young matron in San Augustine County paid twenty-four dollars in late 1862.[13] Of course, Southerners found ready-made commercial clothing, when available, even more dear. Texan Franklin Barlow Sexton, in Richmond, Virginia, as a Confederate congressman in April, 1863, wrote with pained wonder of a similar purchase in his diary: "Got a suit of clothes today (i.e.—coat & pants only) which cost $120. Think of that! My conscience. It is too common grey cassimere. What is to become of the Country. I am almost sorry I got the goods."[14]

But as the war dragged on, cloth—much less a ready-made suit—was simply not to be had. Gradually people in the more established areas of Texas had as great a need for fabric as the most far-flung frontier families, but they often lacked their skills and resources.

At least one emigrant professional weaver offered his services; B. Femelat, identified as "a practical weaver . . . having been employed in the manufactories at Lyons, France," offered in the *Dallas Herald* in November, 1862, to make cloth at the charge of "one-seventh of the cloth" or "25 cts. for single width & 50 cts. for double width."[15]

Initially, the more affluent tried "hiring neighbor women to weave cloth," at least for slave apparel, but few women in established areas had the time or skill to devote to production weaving.[16] In areas where the old skills were still practiced, those needing clothes and linens might barter for homemade textiles; Czech settlers obtained cloth from Anglo-American women in exchange for their home-grown tobacco, which the Anglo women sent to their men in the army. Or the bartering might take the form of sharing in clothing production; M. E. Austin of Colorado County wrote in 1864 to her friend Sarah Perry, "If you only saw how busy I am. Last week, I sewed for a woman in the neighborhood who will weave for me in return."[17]

Many families improvised as long as possible by making clothing out of old sacks and other fabric that had been used for different purposes. A Czech emigrant who settled near New Ulm in 1861, Anna Mikeska Holik, "ripped the covering from the feather beds brought from the Old Country and made shirts for the children as long as the material lasted."[18]

When even these measures could not be employed, home textile production became as much of a patriotic activity for women as it had during the American Revolution. Lena Dancy Ledbetter, who as a fourteen-year-old girl on her parents' Texas plantation in 1864 spun, wove, and sewed her own black-and-white basket-weave dress, would cite the chorus of the Confederate song "Bonny Blue Flag":

> *My homespun dress is plain I know,*
> *My fan is homemade too*
> *But then it shows what Southern girls*
> *For Southern Rights will do.*
> *Hurrah! Hurrah! for the Bonnie Blue flag hurrah!*
> *Hurrah for our Southern rights*
> *And for our Southern boys!*[19]

Texas government officials and other state and community leaders from the beginning of the war promoted such sentiments and the productivity of the women and girls that they represented. As Ralph Wooster explains, "Newspaper editors encouraged home weaving, competition between women was encouraged, and Governor Francis R. Lubbock was inaugurated in a homespun suit in 1861."[20]

But a number of obstacles to widespread home textile production quickly became apparent. For one thing, cotton crops fell off during the war, and the Confederate government considered what was produced to be too economically and politically valuable to be set aside for domestic manufacture. Men could and did make fortunes smuggling the "white gold" through Mexico, farmers and planters used it for barter as "Confederate paper money dropped in value," and the government tried to regulate its movement and sale in order to influence England and France to side with the South.[21]

Given the responsibility of clothing soldiers and families but not given access to the cotton, women became aggressive. A Civil War resident of Belton would recall, "Our cotton that we used for the manufacture of clothing we obtained by the women going out and stopping the government wagons and confiscating what cotton we needed under protest from the drivers."[22]

Similarly, cotton and wool cards were difficult to obtain; San Augustine families in 1862 gratefully accepted a neighbor's offer "to go to Matamoros to buy cards and other necessities." Cards in Texas sold for twenty-five, even forty dollars a pair; as they did with the cotton, Belton women acted on the information that six hundred pairs of cotton cards had arrived in town for sale. "The women just went down and demanded that the cards be given to them as they had to have them and had no money to pay for them. This was done though with grumbling consent."[23]

County governments also stepped in. Among the actions of Kaufman County's commissioners' court in 1863 were the apportioning of money "to cover the expenses in the purchase of 113 Jr. cotton cards" and the authorizing of a trip to Huntsville by a county official "to draw cotton cards from penitentiary." In Jack County on August 3 of the same year, the court met to distribute cards; nineteen

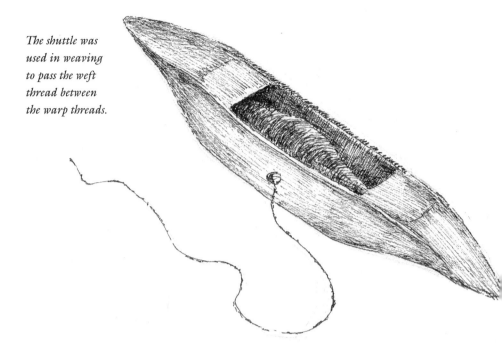

The shuttle was used in weaving to pass the weft thread between the warp threads.

people (listed as female, male, or simply by family name) received both wool and cotton cards for a payment of $12.50, while four received wool cards only at $6.50 a pair.[24]

No record has been uncovered of spinning wheels or looms being imported into Texas during the Civil War, but local manufacture by carpenters and sometime-carpenters continued. B. Femelat, in addition to offering his weaving services to Dallas citizens, advertised in late 1862 that he was building looms with fly shuttles for sale.[25] (The fly shuttle, invented in 1733 and used by professional weavers, had an apparatus that fit across the warp; the weaver would pull a lever, and the shuttle, made like a boat shuttle, would "fly" across the warp threads from a box at one end of the apparatus to a box at the other end.)

Texans desperately depended upon fiber and tools of the home textile trade, most aptly demonstrated by Ottilie Goeth's explanation that "one turned again to spinning and weaving in order not to go about in rags" and by a young woman's report that on a late 1862 visit to Nacogdoches "everywhere she went 'she saw hanks of thread hanging about the house.'"[26] Women and girls had to produce material for themselves, for their families, and for the Confederate war effort, so that the soldiers would not "go about in rags" either.

Again, children often helped. Sallie Haltom of Tarrant County would recall her family using ginned cotton, but when that supply was depleted, the "long drive" to the cotton gin made it necessary for the children to "hand [pick] enough lint for next days spinning on the spinning wheel." Even in the family of Matthew Cartwright, prominent San Augustine "Land Trader" and sixth richest man in the state in 1860, by early 1863 the younger children had learned how to spin cotton and eighteen-year-old Anna could weave.[27]

The widespread effort differed from previous Texas home textile activity and from the continuing pioneer activity in that women had to resurrect rusty skills or, more commonly, to develop these skills very quickly from scratch. Mary Maverick of San Antonio had grown up the daughter of an Alabama plantation family but apparently had never been involved at this level of home textile production. In January, 1863, she reported to one of her Confederate soldier sons that relatives on the Cibolo were "all making homespun down there" and that she "took lessons in spinning & showed quite a genius for carding and spinning."[28] She obtained a spinning wheel, but most of her textile activity during the war seemed to be knitting and sewing. Meanwhile, a member of the Maverick household, slave Jinny Anderson, spun thread on the wheel for soldiers' socks.

Jinny was an elderly woman, the nurse for Mary's husband Sam during his childhood. Although the historical record obscures their contributions, older slave women

probably knew how to spin and weave from past experience and continued to do so as deemed necessary by plantation owners. Aside from carrying on the traditions of the
far frontier, these pioneer women were most likely to
have these skills and to use or pass them along. Abigail
Holbrook notes, "When war forced the women to return
to the spinning wheels and looms, a number of Negro
women were familiar with the whirl of the wheel. Each November, for instance, [the female slaves on one plantation]
had been testing their skill at night by spinning threads for
plow-lines. However, the art of spinning was not a common one."[29]

If some slave women had maintained their skills, others, like their Anglo counterparts, had to start anew with
the intricacies of cloth making. Matthew Cartwright's wife
Amanda in late 1862 "decided to buy a loom and have
some of the slave women learn to weave."[30]

Again, the division of labor between female slaves and
female members of the slaveholding family varied from
household to household. A Bell County resident, Eugenia
Haldeman Openheimer, would recall that during the war
"we spun and wove the clothes worn by the servants but
were fortunate enough to have calico and muslin for our-
selves," the fabric brought from Mexico. On one South
Texas plantation, slaves spun and dyed for all, but a female
relative of the owner's family, her husband away fighting,
came for the duration and did the weaving. On the Thomas
Speake plantation in Lavaca County, Mrs. Speake in 1864
produced a still-extant child's shirt and pants using the
plantation's cultivated indigo and cotton, but whether she
meant the outfit for a slave child or a member of the family
is unclear.[31]

On Jon and Lucy Dancy's Fayette County plantation,
everyone resorted to homespun, but the Dancy women

"refused to let any one of [the] slaves spin their favorite dresses." Still, daughter Lena indicated the scope and skill of the slave women, writing, "All our blankets, towels and negro clothes were spun & woven by his [Jon Dancy's] spinners, and they were willing experts" who produced a variety of patterns. Lena indicates that black and white women worked together in this enterprise, noting, "Some of these patterns were difficult to put through the sley [reed], but each one of us made an effort to do the work well."[32]

The need to produce homespun sent Jon Dancy and others with large slave forces scrambling for equipment. Dancy rounded up thirteen wheels, two reels, and a loom and established a "Loom House" beside the "Negro nursery." Rebecca Adams of Freestone County wrote her husband in the Confederacy in late 1863 that her father had gone to Hempstead to obtain wheels and looms to employ fifty slave women on his own plantation. On the Adams plantation, Rebecca was working at a loom trying to "get the negroes some clothes made before cold weather," as "there is no other way to clothe the negroes but to make the cloth at home."[33]

Rebecca Adams's industry is typical of women left to run things at home, whether on a plantation, a small family farm, or an urban site. War always brought extra responsibilities to be shouldered by women on the home front. Many women of nineteenth-century Texas had had plenty of training, for the menfolk often traveled extensively on various forms of business, absenting themselves from home for long periods. But as the war dragged into months and years, women had to become even more self-sufficient and resourceful, both in meeting their own family's needs and in supplying the Confederate soldiers. Typical was Martha Speaks Vaughn of Menard County: "[Martha] was left to manage the home, to look after the welfare of the children, to manage crops and herds, to dispose of the surplus products as best she could. In addition to this, she worked all day and many times far into the night, carding and spinning and weaving the wool into thread and then into cloth."[34] This cloth was used both for the family and for Confederate soldiers. "I was a girl of fifteen when the Civil War began," Amzina Wade would recall. "I carded and spun thread to be woven into jeans, flannel, and blankets, to clothe our Southern soldiers."[35]

Women commonly donated their homemade cloth or processed it into completed clothing for the war effort. Stephen B. Oates demonstrates how necessary and significant women's support efforts were by pointing out that the Confederate government in Richmond "could barely supply its armies in Virginia," while the Texas government "was equally incompetent." Soldiers had to fend for themselves, but he notes, "probably their largest source of quartermaster stores was the innumerable women's committees that began to be formed around the state almost concurrently with the raising of the first regiments."[36]

Sarah Crist Chaffin, a Texas native who had learned "to card and to spin and to weave" as a girl, not only raised flax and spun and wove her own fine linen but also "had her sheep sheared and spun the wool into thread, then wove it into cloth, the cloth being used for uniforms for the Confederate soldiers." Juliet Smith McClelland, who arrived in Texas in 1846 with her husband and nine children, during the war spun and wove and directed her slaves in textile production so that she could provide a "warm suit of clothes" to passing soldiers.[37] (Ironically, slaves often contributed to the Confederate effort in this way—Lizzie Atkins of Washington County would recall, "Maser had all of us using the spinning wheel and making clothes for the

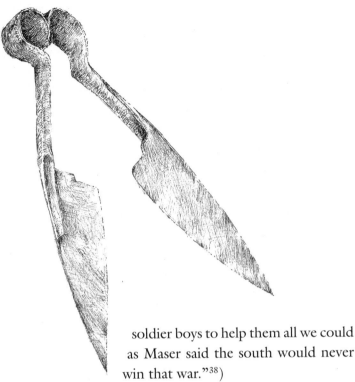

soldier boys to help them all we could as Maser said the south would never win that war."[38])

Sarah Ellen Eaton McCallister of Coryell County also became heavily involved in supplying soldiers, although one might wonder, as with the slaves, how voluntary were some of her efforts. Husband David was inclined to press "his own homespun blankets and clothing" upon "less fortunate companions in arms," then ask for more; Sarah and her daughters "sometimes sat up all night spinning and weaving to make him more blankets and clothing."[39]

Even the most casual appeal doubtless stimulated activity—and guilt. In May, 1862, Hiram Brown wrote his sister Sarah Perry from a Texas Confederate camp, "Has Mrs. Lathrop sent down anything to you for Burrell[?] He is out of clothes & tho't that she might have sent down some for Lewis too."[40]

Sallie Reynolds Matthews tells a dramatic story of providing soldiers' clothing in *Interwoven,* the story reflecting both pioneer women's expertise and Civil War realities. Texas's far western frontier—the settlers inhabiting the north central prairies and oak forests and the western edge of the central Texas hill country—became increasingly exposed to Indian raids as the Texas government concentrated on the state's role in the war. Frontier defense weakened to the point that many families had to "fort up" together, and many were killed or abducted by Comanches. In the Elm Creek Raid of 1864 in Young County, unlike some of their neighbors, Mrs. Billy Bragg and her children escaped murder or kidnapping, but the Comanches ransacked the home and took a suit Mrs. Bragg had just completed for her son in the Confederacy. She had planned to send the suit to him by a relative ending his furlough in the area.

Mrs. Bragg prevailed upon the relative to get his furlough extended. The Comanches had overlooked her raw wool and ignored her spinning wheel, cards, and loom. In the next ten days, Matthews relates, Mrs. Bragg "worked night and day" spinning, washing, dyeing, weaving, even knitting socks, "at intervals taking a nap on [the raw] wool in front of the fire," and had the suit ready to send with the relative.[41]

Another intriguing story combining frontier textile know-how and industry with Civil War realities involves two men, Blanco County farmers Jap Brown and John C. Pierce. The two chose to hide in a cave near the Brown farm rather than join the Confederate forces. In constant contact with Brown's wife, they were often sought for conscription by the Home Guard but were never found. The men passed much of their time spinning by the light of tallow candles, a skill that they had apparently learned as boys, and "the vast amount of spun thread carried from

the cave under cover of darkness was a prime factor in causing people to wonder how it was that Mrs. Brown made
more cloth than any two women in the country."[42]

Whatever the circumstances of textile production, little
attention could be paid to beauty in these years; as one
woman wrote looking back on her Civil War days, "The
coarse fabrics then were a far cry from the delicate and ex-
quisite weaves of today." But an aesthetic dimension remained. A description of the home dyeing of Mildred
Satterwhite Littlefield of Gonzales County during the war
has a romantic cast but nonetheless reflects the pleasure of
working with yarn and color: "[She] took her own cotton
and wool, made dyes from moss, weeds, and minerals from
the earth on her place, and created 'pretty, rich, soft, firm,
strong, comfortable cloth of all kinds and in as many colors
as Joseph's coat.'"[43]

Lena Dancy Ledbetter also gave testimony to the art
of creating cloth; she reported using weaving books for
patterns on the Dancy plantation and recorded in a booklet of her own "Patterns for Weaving Counterpanes &c
1862–1865."[44] A few striking overshot coverlets made in
Texas during the war still exist in museum collections.

Whether or not the cloth had beauty, women still exhibited a satisfaction in home production. Ledbetter spoke
proudly of the burial suit of her father, who died shortly
after the war ended; her mother had made the suit in 1864
using wool sheared from the sheep in the Dancy pastures,
spun and woven by the Dancy slaves, and dyed from bark
from the plantation's trees.

Throughout this era, spinners and weavers continued
to do their work very much as previous generations had.
Ironically, with some sewing machines already in use in Texas
at the beginning of the war, women found themselves in a
curious time warp—producing the cloth in the laborious

manner their ancestors had, but having the machine technology to speed the actual construction at the end. A memory of German emigrant Emilie Ploeger Schumann of Round Top reflects the value of that technology: "Toward the end of the War, my great-grandmother had only one needle left for her sewing machine. She would not let her daughters use the machine; for if the needle was broken, she would be unable to sew what was needed."[45]

The war propelled Texas and the whole South into attempts to industrialize. A visit to a carding factory operating in McLennan County in 1862 caused one spinner, Tennessee Embree, to exclaim in her diary, "It is truly a great invention. I think what a world of genius is this!"[46]

Even better, of course, would be cotton and wool mills providing a steady supply of fabric. The state government during the war offered a "half section of the public domain" for a thousand dollars' worth of "new and efficient machinery" for various manufacturing uses, including the conversion of "cotton or wool into thread or cloth."[47] Meanwhile, Huntsville penitentiary inmates continued to produce cloth in their mill—more than two hundred prisoners "turn[ing] out nearly 6,000 yards of cloth daily," some of it bought by counties to provide for soldiers' families.[48]

The drop in prison population during the war hurt Huntsville production, as did the lack of replacement parts and skilled workers "to manufacture the parts and needed supplies." (By the end of the war, slaves were being used as production workers in the Huntsville mill.) But the operation had proven a success, for "textile mill profits were the largest single source of income for the state . . . during the Civil War, accounting for thirty-eight percent of the state's total net receipts."[49]

Meanwhile, the government was encouraging other mill

efforts. The Comal Manufacturing Company of New Braunfels, in Comal County, received a charter in 1863 to produce cotton and woolen goods, but the power looms ordered from Europe did not arrive via Matamoros until early 1865.

As the national conflict shuddered to an end, the deprivations of the war years and the bitterness of defeat caused riotous scenes, such as the one in Houston when the soldiers there disbanded in May, 1865, and, "joined by men, women, and children," raided government stores of fabric and clothing. One observer saw "mounted soldiers riding up and down the streets trailing open bolts of cloth behind them."[50]

After the war, population jumped "as a result of [renewed] heavy migration from the older South," supply routes were reestablished, and trade flourished to the point that bankers and merchants quickly replaced in power the old plantation aristocracy. Commercial textiles originating in Europe and the Northeast became readily available in most areas of Texas. Calico that had sold for as much as twenty-five dollars a yard by the early 1870s was being sold in San Antonio "25 yards to the dollar, and merchants used it in place of brown paper for wrapping purposes."[51]

The penitentiary mill declined after the war, and the Comal Manufacturing Company started out vigorously in 1865 but could not rebound from flood and tornado damage in 1869. The 1870 census showed "four flourishing mills . . . three of which used Texas cotton exclusively."[52] The New Braunfels Woolen Manufacturing Company, established in 1868, "turned out forty pairs of blankets and two hundred yards of tweeds or yarns a day."[53] But by 1880, neither this nor the other three operations were listed.

Still, these Texas manufacturing efforts and the resumption and development of mercantile trade with the Northeast and foreign countries enabled women to retire wheel, loom, and dye pot for good. And most gladly did, concentrating their textile activity primarily on sewing, knitting, and quilting, with the quilts sometimes boasting the old and increasingly rare homespun pieces.

But the preindustrial patterns remained on the frontier, as evidenced by Mrs. J. J. Greenwood's recollections of settling in Lampasas, Lampasas County, after the war. Most area homes were constructed of logs, with wood shutters rather than glass windows. Women made their own lye soap, stuffed mattresses with corn shucks, and cooked in the fireplace with heavy iron pots. Families produced their evening light "by first killing a beef to obtain the tallow, then rendering and molding it [into candles], and even spinning the wicks." Mrs. Greenwood wove cloth and, lacking a sewing machine, handsewed her husband a wool and cotton suit. "It was not at all a bad looking suit for that day and time," she wrote, "and I marvel now when I look back and wonder how I did it."[54]

As the state came out of the throes of Reconstruction, a number of factors—rapid population increase, suppression of the Comanches, the growth of ranching, general economic development, transportation improvements, technological innovations, the continuing lure of raw land— led settlers into the brush country of Southwest Texas and onto the mesquite savannas sweeping northward through West Texas. Pioneer accounts from the 1870s and 1880s— diaries, letters, and memoirs—repeatedly refer to women's sewing, seldom if at all touching on production of yarn or cloth, although the boom in sheep and goat ranching made fiber easily available for many. Some frontier women of the post–Civil War era continued to spin thread for knitting, but one West Texas settler who had carried her wheel with her couldn't obtain the cotton for spinning and eventually traded the wheel for a "fine, large female pig."[55]

Yet the traditions did not completely die. The various small wool-carding businesses in Texas in 1870 were no doubt being patronized by home spinners. The 1870 census still identified women scattered across Texas as spinners and weavers by occupation.[56] Diane Greene Taylor's 1977 statewide survey of nineteenth-century textiles identified the existence of equipment that indicates a continuing tradition, such as the flax wheel made in 1875 and used by the Erickson family in Krum. Further, it identified a few surviving coverlets produced in 1870s Texas, indicating that that craft survived when necessity no longer made the creation of linens imperative.

By 1880, home spinning and especially home weaving had declined to the point where most Texas residents considered these activities quaint and outmoded. The activities did not disappear entirely; Taylor's survey found "partial home weavers and even a few professionals . . . still producing cloth" in the 1880s, during the time that the Sanctificationist women of Belton were supporting their all-female communal enterprise in part by weaving rag rugs.[57]

Further, as Texas became increasingly urban and increasingly dependent on manufactured goods, some rural dwellers continued to adhere to old traditions of self-reliance. Lack of money was a factor. C. C. White would recall his mother's and his own spinning activity during his boyhood in the East Texas piney woods in the 1890s: "We could a bought thread at the store, they had what they called 'ball thread,' that looked something like balls of wrapping cord, only it was fine. But we didn't have no money. Most folks didn't have no money."[58]

But one also gets the sense from rural reminiscences of

the time that families' adherence to textile traditions went beyond simple economic considerations. Mary Ellen Flowers Walker, a native Texan, remembered of life in the Big Thicket in the 1880s, "We made all our clothes, the thread, the cloth, all by hand." There were no shortcuts in Mary Ellen's world; her family grew cotton, picked the seed out by hand, obtained wool from a neighbor's sheep, and picked it by hand also. Family members carded and spun, "made cloth on grandma's old loom," and raised their own indigo bushes for dye. "You let 'em get about three feet high and they'd ring 'em, pack 'em in a barrel and pour water over 'em. Let 'em set there in that water till it begins to foam on top. They'd take a hoe then and churn it, then after [a] while the indigo mud would come up just like butter on milk. They'd take that out and lay it up and let it dry. They'd dye blue with it, the prettiest blue you ever did see." The degree of self-reliant resourcefulness exhibited not only by Mary Ellen's family but also by her community is further reflected in her memory of the annual community summer revivals lasting a week or two, girls "dye[ing] their dresses two or three different colors" as the revival progressed so that it would appear they had a larger wardrobe.[59]

While Mary Ellen would as an old woman speak with relish of these textile activities, no doubt many women gratefully left behind such extended labor. Unlike the furniture, tools, buildings, and stone fences crafted by the menfolk, the cloth they had created often did not survive them. Of searching out clothing for the historical exhibits of the 1936 Texas Centennial Exposition, Mary Reid wrote, "The most difficult things to locate were a buckskin suit and a homespun dress."[60]

The swatches that do occasionally surface, the fading coverlets that do make their way into museum collection or antique store, tell us much about the lives of a large number of women in the developing Anglo-dominated Texas of the nineteenth century. First, they show how slowly the old subsistence patterns passed away—more slowly in Texas than in most other settled regions of nineteenth-century America. Portions of Texas remained a frontier for many years, due to continuing volatile relations with the Native Americans and with Mexico, to Texas' own uncertain economic and political status, and to an isolation fed by Texas' distance from eastern centers, its vast size, its challenging terrains, and the halting growth of transportation and industry.

The surviving fabrics also remind us how firmly gender roles remained in place as Texas developed in the nineteenth century. Men and children, male and female, performed a number of textile-related tasks, but with very few exceptions, women and girls were the spinners and the weavers, the dyers and knitters, working in the ancient tradition of home as factory. While women of independent yeoman farming families and slave women on large plantations performed the most textile production work, women at all socioeconomic levels were involved, especially during the Civil War.

The faded pieces further remind us that this involvement took great amounts of women's time, skill, and labor. While textile production activity had to be burdensome to many, it also fostered community and brought genuine satisfactions. Families worked together; black and white women worked together; women and girls in other frontier communities worked together, often with assistance from male community members.

And whether working together or alone, many women clearly enjoyed the peaceful, rhythmic nature of twisting thread and throwing shuttle and took pleasure in meeting the clothing and linen needs of family and friends. The beauty of much of the yarn and cloth produced lay only in their durability. But spinning, weaving, and dyeing offered a range of creative possibilities, even when fiber choices were limited. Plying the thread, trying a different dye plant or mordant, adding more threads per vertical inch to the warp, experimenting with different harness combinations, alternating colored and plain yarn in warp or weft—all yielded new and sometimes delightful results. The simplest checked pattern as it grew upon the loom had a crisp utilitarian beauty, while coverlets, like quilts, represented the artistry and technical skill of their makers. Through home textile production, nineteenth-century Texas women reasserted their role as essential home producer and demonstrated an ability to make art of the rough fiber of everyday existence in a remote Mexican province, a tenuous republic, and a growing state.

This white cotton homespun, hand-woven wedding dress, about 1845, belonged to Sarah Tate, slave of the Edgar family of De Witt County. The dress was reportedly "made for her" by her young mistress, which demonstrates a close bond between them. Courtesy of San Antonio Museum Association. Photo by James T. Hershorn.

Cleveland Doss in 1917 modeled the dress Lena Dancy Ledbetter made for herself from spinning to sewing on the Dancy plantation during the Civil War. Courtesy of Center for American History, University of Texas at Austin (Lena Dancy Ledbetter Collection CN 06266).

*This overshot
coverlet, produced
by slaves in
Jefferson County,
about 1840,
illustrates that
slave women were
involved in the
finer aspects
of textile pro-
duction as well as
the strictly utili-
tarian produc-
tion of cloth.*
Courtesy of
San Antonio Mu-
seum Association.
Photo by
James T.
Hershorn.

During the Civil War, Lena Dancy kept a booklet she titled "Patterns for Weaving Counterpanes &c"; this "Nine Snowballs" pattern draft from it shows how to thread the loom and when to raise which harnesses. Courtesy of Center for American History, University of Texas at Austin (Lena Dancy Ledbetter Collection CN 06258).

Weaving patterns for the Loom.

Nine Snowballs draft

This draft answers for wool or Cotton.
When you commince weaving, tread the second spot
marked 2nd which will cause the snowball to be round)

End

Stephen F. Austin's land plat book is covered in homespun believed to be produced by a female member of Austin's family. Courtesy of Center for American History.

In the late nine-teenth century, Texas women were quilting with inexpensive fabric and with scraps, some of the latter homespun. Here, a version of the Dresden Plate design, created in Shelby County, about 1885–90, is pieced in large part of homespun fabrics.
Courtesy of San Antonio Museum Association.
Photo by James T. Hershorn.

This overshot coverlet was passed down through a branch of Sam Houston's family and was said to have been produced by wife Margaret or by his mother. Courtesy of Gillespie County Historical Society. Photo by James T. Hershorn.

More girls and women were involved in the knitting of socks than in any other textile activity. Mrs. Rumke, an early New Braunfels settler, knitted these lacy socks for a little girl about 1860. Courtesy of San Antonio Museum Association. Photo by James T. Hershorn.

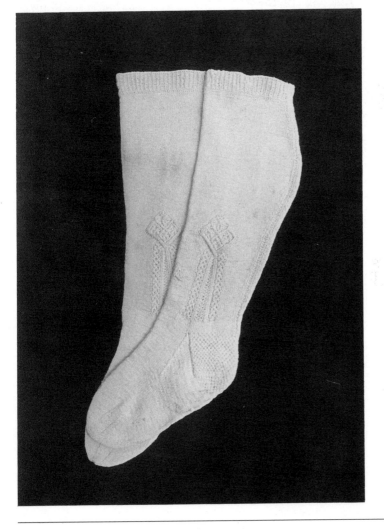

During the Civil War, Gertrude Etelinger of Gonzales made these for Peter Etelinger, a member of the First Texas Regiment of Hood's Brigade. Courtesy of San Antonio Museum Association. Photo by James T. Hershorn.

Notes

INTRODUCTION

1. In *Hecho en Tejas: Texas Mexican Folk Arts and Crafts,* Joe S. Graham states, "If one depended on museum collections, one might conclude that the Hispanics in the region had no weaving tradition at all," p. 25. Of course, the limited number of surviving European-American- and African-American-produced textiles might lead to an erroneous conclusion as well, but the women producers still enter the dominant culture's historical record, however fleetingly.

CHAPTER ONE

1. In particular, many English and Scotch-Irish families emigrated with a "strong linen-making heritage." See Judith Reiter Weissman and Wendy Lavitt, *Labors of Love: America's Textiles and Needlework, 1650–1930,* p. 4.

2. Alice Morse Earle, *Home Life in Colonial Days,* p. 211; Jean H. Baker, *Mary Todd Lincoln: A Biography,* p. 14.

3. Jared Van Wagenen Jr., *The Golden Age of Homespun,* p. 249.

4. Earle, *Home Life,* p. 167.

5. Laurel Thatcher Ulrich, *Good Wives: Image and Reality in the Lives of Women in Northern New England, 1650–1750,* p. 29.

6. Ibid., pp. 179–80; Anne L. MacDonald, *No Idle Hands: The Social History of American Knitting,* p. 6; Mary Frost Steen, "To Utilize Every Idle Hand: Silk Culture in the United States," *Spin-Off* 18, no. 2 (Summer, 1994): 108.

7. Weissman and Lavitt, *Labors of Love,* p. 7.

8. Earle, *Home Life,* pp. 169, 171.

9. R. Carlyle Buley, *The Old Northwest Pioneer Period, 1815–1840,* vol. 1, p. 204; Dona Price, personal notes provided to author, June 11, 1994, p. 1.

10. Jack Larkin in *The Reshaping of Everyday Life* indicates that ethnicity and region made a difference in how the work was divided. German-American women and women in eastern Pennsylvania were reported participating in some of the flax operations usually performed by men—the separating and spreading of fibers and the breaking and swingling; John Mack Faragher, "The Midwestern Farming Family, 1850," in *Women's America: Refocusing the Past,* ed. Linda K. Kerber and Jane Sherron De Hart, p. 54.

11. Marcia Bonta, "Eliza Lucas Pinckney, Cultivator of Indigo," in *Dyes from Nature,* ed. Rita Buchanan, p. 33.

12. See Rose T. Briggs, "Plymouth Colony's Dye Plants," in *Dye Plants and Dyeing—A Handbook.* Briggs's article has formed the basis of my discussion of colonial dyestuffs.

13. Debbie Redding, *Learning to Weave with Debbie Redding,* p. 213.

14. Price, personal notes, p. 2.

15. Redding, *Learning to Weave,* p. 213.

16. Ibid., p. 123; Jane Parker, "Glossary of Fabrics Common in 19th Century Texas," in "Institute of Texan Cultures Final Report, Summer 1988—Early Texas Textiles," n.p.

17. Carol Strickler, *American Woven Coverlets,* p. 26, 80–81. Some patterns—including the more complex overshots—required more harnesses and thus were the province of professional weavers.

18. Earle, *Home Life,* p. 227.

19. MacDonald, *No Idle Hands,* pp. 26–27.

20. Earle, *Home Life,* pp. 183–84; Julia Cherry Spruill, *Women's Life and Work in the Southern Colonies,* pp. 74–76.

21. Quoted in Earle, *Home Life,* p. 185, no source given.

22. Earle, *Home Life,* pp. 204–5; Van Wagenen, *Golden Age of Homespun,* p. 265.

23. Earle, *Home Life,* p. 208.

24. Susan Strasser, *Never Done: A History of American Housework,* p. 128.

25. Ibid., p. 126; see Frances Louisa Goodrich, *Mountain Homespun,* p. 4. Thomas Jefferson saw in home textile production one of the best promises of freedom from dependence on England, so that "the articles we shall in future want from them will not exceed their own consumption of our produce."

26. Strasser, *Never Done,* p. 129; estimates of the end of the "age of homespun" in the Northeast vary. Larkin in *Reshaping of Everyday Life*

says that "by 1830, the loom and wool wheel had begun to disappear" and "within a decade country families were consigning their textile equipment to the attic." Van Wagenen indicates that the availability of factory-produced cotton warp helped extend the home weaving tradition in New York state and shows home production continuing into the 1840s.

27. This is a standard interpretation. For a fuller discussion, see Sarah Evans's *Born for Liberty*. For its application to the lives of women on the Texas frontier, see Ann Patton Malone's *Women on the Texas Frontier: A Cross-Cultural Perspective*, pp. 14–25.

28. For a discussion of the tensions between myth and reality, see Catherine Clinton's *The Plantation Mistress*.

29. Former slave Martha King, quoted in Elizabeth Fox-Genovese, *Within the Plantation Household: Black and White Women of the Old South*, p. 178. Fox-Genovese also quotes a former slave who reported that the slave women "could sell the thread they spun at night."

30. Jacqueline Jones, *Labor of Love, Labor of Sorrow: Black Women, Work, and the Family from Slavery to the Present*, p. 31.

31. Sally J. McMillen, *Southern Women: Black and White in the Old South*, p. 101.

32. Strickler, *American Woven Coverlets*, p. 14.

33. Buley, *Old Northwest Pioneer Period*, p. 207.

34. Spruill, *Women's Life & Work*, pp. 81–83.

35. Clyde A. Milner II, "Kitturah Belknap Prepares for the Trip to Oregon, 1847–1848," in *Major Problems in the History of the American West: Documents and Essays*, p. 263.

36. Faragher, "Midwestern Farming Family," p. 69.

37. Francis Parkman reported his traveling party passing a wagon train from Missouri bound for the Far West and creating a sensation: "the careworn, thin-featured matron, or the buxom girl, seated in front [of each wagon] suspended the knitting on which most of them were engaged to stare at us with wondering curiosity." See Frank Bergon and Zeese Papanikolas, "A Boston Intellectual's View," in *Looking Far West: The Search for the American West in History, Myth, and Literature*, p. 204.

38. Quoted in Gail Andrews Trechsel, "Mourning Quilts: That Distress, By Industry, May Be Removed," *Piecework* 2, no. 2 (Mar./Apr., 1994): 54.

39. Bergon and Papanikolas, "Making Do in the Wilderness," in *Looking Far West*, p. 227.

40. David Anders, "Typescript Reminiscences, 1897," p. 2.

41. For example, in "Midwestern Farming Family," Faragher states, "Until the Civil War . . . a good deal of all midwestern clothing, and most clothing on emigrant backs, was homespun" (pp. 54–55).

42. MacDonald, *No Idle Hands,* pp. 121, 123.

43. E. Jane Robison and Jeri Robison-Turner, eds., *Unbroken Circle,* p. 24.

44. The tradition dwindled by 1890 but was resurrected by the "fotched-on women," Protestant cultural missionaries from the Northeast who arrived in the mountains to "uplift" the inhabitants, in part by encouraging women's home industry. See Goodrich, *Mountain Homespun.*

45. Ethel Frances Jones in "The Elixir of Youth" (*Boone County [Arkansas] Historian* 17, no. 1 [Jan./Feb./Mar., 1994]: 5–10) recounted visiting a family deep in the Arkansas Ozarks in the 1880s and finding in the kitchen a spinning wheel and a loom that produced these items. Jones was the daughter of the Elixir Springs postmaster; part of the post office was rented to a merchant who stocked calico, and Jones's family apparently had a ready supply of fabric. The reference to wristbands is on p. 7.

46. Jude Daurelle, "A Place to Come To," *Piecework* 2, no. 3 (May/June, 1994): 11; Steen, "To Utilize Every Idle Hand," pp. 107, 109.

47. Malinda Jenkins, *Gambler's Wife: The Life of Malinda Jenkins,* p. 60. Jenkins had even knit her husband's suspenders.

48. The fragment is at the Witte Museum, San Antonio. See Parker, "Institute of Texas Cultures," p. 4.

49. San Antonio Bicentennial Heritage Committee, *San Antonio in the Eighteenth Century,* p. 40; Graham, *Hecho en Tejas,* pp. 17–18, cites the 1772 inventory of the contents of Mission San Juan Bautista on the Rio Grande.

50. Chloe Sayer in *Arts and Crafts of Mexico* reports cloth supplies coming into Mexico from Spain, the Philippines, and China in the sixteenth century; Parker, "Institute of Texas Cultures," pp. 6–7; San Antonio Bicentennial Heritage Committee, *San Antonio,* p. 81.

51. See Noah Smithwick, *The Evolution of a State or Recollections of Old Texas Days,* p. 34. Smithwick was in "San Fernando," but it is not clear from his account whether this was San Fernando de Béxar (now San Antonio) or another community. Sayer in *Arts and Crafts of Mexico* points out that such a simple loom does offer artistic flexibility, allowing weavers to create varied effects with their manipulation of individual threads.

52. Cecilia Steinfeldt, "Nineteenth Century Textiles in Texas," p. 3.

53. Parker, "Institute of Texas Cultures," p. 4; Dianna Everett, *The Texas Cherokees: A People between Two Fires, 1819–1840,* p. 53.

54. For a possible exception, see the reference to Zavala County weavers in Chapter 3.

CHAPTER TWO

1. Quoted in David Holman and Billie Persons, *Buckskin and Homespun: Frontier Texas Clothing, 1820–1870*, pp. 2–3. It is unclear from this passage whether Austin expected his mother and sister to produce or obtain homespun, but the family was from frontier Missouri, where spinning and weaving were still quite common activities among women.

2. Larkin, *Reshaping of Everyday Life*, p. 50; *Texas Gazette*, Texas Newspaper Files, Center for American History.

3. Larkin points out that "industrial production made far greater quantities of fabric available," giving women the capability of making "shirts, dresses, curtains, bedspreads, sheets and towels in greater numbers than their grandmothers had done" (*Reshaping of Everyday Life*, p. 50).

4. Annie Doom Pickrell, ed., *Pioneer Women in Texas*, p. 216.

5. Ibid., p. 240.

6. Smithwick, *The Evolution of a State*, p. 5. I could find no indication that early settlers attempted to use the wild flax and wild hemp that grew in Texas, although they certainly may have experimented with these fiber sources.

7. Letter of Dec. 21, 1832, Perry Papers, Center for American History, Austin; in January, 1833, San Felipe merchant Joshua Fletcher complained to James Franklin Perry that business was "dull"—"I have none of the leading articles neither Coffee Shoes or ready made cloathin[,] articles which are most in demand" (typescript letter of Jan. 18, 1833, Perry Papers).

8. Letter to "MESSRS. PRINTERS," *Texas Gazette*, [Mar. 1930 edition?], Center for American History.

9. Hermann Seele, *The Cypress and Other Writings of a German Pioneer in Texas*, p. 62. Steinfeldt in "Nineteenth Century Textiles" mentions Eugenie Lavender, "an aristocratic, sophisticated lady artist who had come to Texas from France in the 1850s," wearing a buckskin coat and trousers, but Lavender no doubt had other sartorial choices.

10. Rabb's memoirs are included in Jo Ella Powell Exley, ed., *Texas Tears and Texas Sunshine: Voices of Frontier Women*, pp. 5–18.

11. Ibid., pp. 9, 12.

12. Ibid., p. 13.

13. Ibid., pp. 14–15.

14. Ibid., p. 18.

15. Betty J. Mills, *Calico Chronicle*, p. 19.

16. Laurel Thatcher Ulrich's *A Midwife's Tale: The Life of Martha Ballard Based on Her Diary, 1785–1812* won the Pulitzer Prize and

provides a fascinating, multilayered look at an "average" woman's life.

17. Pickrell, *Pioneer Women in Texas,* p. 360.

18. Daniel Shipman, *Frontier Life: 58 Years in Texas,* pp. 36–37.

19. Pickrell, *Pioneer Women in Texas,* p. 318; Dilue Harris, "The Reminiscences of Mrs. Dilue Harris," *Quarterly of the Texas State Historical Association* 4, no. 1 (July, 1900): 99–100. Harris mentions that some "made their ropes out of hides and the hair from the manes and tails of horses."

20. Sarah Harkey Hall, *Surviving on the Texas Frontier: The Journal of a Frontier Orphan Girl in San Saba County* (forthcoming).

21. John Michael Vlach, "Afro-American Folk Crafts in Nineteenth Century Texas," *Western Folklore* 40, no. 2 (Apr., 1981), p. 161. My thanks to Sylvia Grider for alerting me to this article, which articulated my own conclusions regarding slave craftsmanship on Texas plantations.

22. Quoted in George P. Rawick, ed., "Texas Narratives, Part 1," in *The American Slave: A Composite Autobiography,* p. 261. Interviewers from the Works Progress Administration in the 1930s produced often exaggerated records of African-American dialect when recording the words of elderly former slaves. For example, it is standard English to pronounce "clothes" as "cloz," but only an interviewer intent on showing his or her subject as unlettered would spell it "close" in the transcript. Despite this reflected bias, for consistency and accuracy to the record itself, I have followed the published spellings from the WPA narratives.

23. See Gladys-Marie Fry, *Stitched from the Soul: Slave Quilts from the Ante-Bellum South,* p. 22; Malone, *Women on the Texas Frontier,* p. 31. From the colonial period, plantation owners tried to build a skilled work force in this regard. The governor of South Carolina in 1745 hired and sent home two Irish servants, a weaver and a spinner. Further, the governor instructed his daughter to "order a Sensible Negroe woman or two to learn to spin, and wheels to be made for them," as he surmised—correctly—that "one Spinner can't keep a Loom at work." See Earle, *Home Life,* pp. 182–83.

24. Fry, *Stitched from the Soul,* p. 61.

25. Quoted in Vlach, "Afro-American Folk Crafts," p. 151.

26. Pickrell, *Pioneer Women in Texas,* p. 13.

27. Ibid., p. 146.

28. Mary Maverick in Paula Mitchell Marks, *Turn Your Eyes toward Texas: Pioneers Sam and Mary Maverick,* p. 176.

29. Pickrell, *Pioneer Women in Texas,* p. 394.

30. Ibid., p. 60.

31. Malone, *Women on the Texas Frontier,* p. 28.

32. Pickrell, *Pioneer Women in Texas,* p. 117.

33. Ibid., p. 417.

34. Ibid., p. 13.

35. Ibid., p. 315; Fry, in *Stitched from the Soul*, remarks, "it should be noted that the bulk of textile production in the antebellum South was accomplished by the labor of slave men and women" (pp. 27, 215).

36. See Terry G. Jordan, *German Seed in Texas Soil: Immigrant Farmers in Nineteenth-Century Texas*, pp. 24–25; Crystal Sasse Ragsdale, ed., *The Golden Free Land: The Reminiscences and Letters of Women on an American Frontier*, p. 12. Kathy Jo Anderson in her "Texas Migration and Immigration" shows some of the ways in which European emigrant women faced greater adaptive challenges than their "migrant" contemporaries.

37. Ragsdale, *The Golden Free Land*, p. 12.

38. "'This Feeble Circle of Light': Lighting Devices in Nineteenth Century Texas," *Star of the Republic Museum Notes* 15, no. 3 (Spring, 1991): n.p.

39. Ibid.

40. Ibid.

41. David B. Edward, *The History of Texas Or The Emigrant's, Farmer's & Politician's Guide to the Character, Climate, Soil & Productions of That Country*, p. 51; Mills, *Calico Chronicle*, p. 21; Holman and Persons, *Buckskin and Homespun*, p. 30.

42. Edward, *The History of Texas*, pp. 41, 43; quoted in Holman and Persons, *Buckskin and Homespun*, p. 41.

43. Delena Tull, *A Practical Guide to Edible and Useful Plants*, p. 350; Edward in his 1836 account says, "The nopal, or prickly-pear, deserves a passing notice, as it is the vegetable which is fed on by the insect that yields the cochineal dye" (p. 43). He later mentions the cultivation of the cochineal by natives.

44. Mills, *Calico Chronicle*, p. 19.

45. Modern dyers have produced bold, varied colors with natural dyes, but nineteenth-century home dyers usually had little in the way of time, opportunity, and resources to develop the craft.

46. Jordan, *German Seed in Texas Soil*, p. 25; Smithwick, *The Evolution of a State*, p. 75.

47. Evelyn M. Carrington, ed., *Women in Early Texas*, pp. 25–26.

CHAPTER THREE

1. To gain a good general idea of the movement of settlement and of vegetation regions, see the maps on pages 23 and 28 of Terry Jordan's *German Seed in Texas Soil*.

2. Ibid., p. 27; Malone, *Women on the Texas Frontier*, p. 21.

3. Anderson, "Texas Migration and Immigration," p. 4.

4. German settlers did continue to use wool and grow flax for domestic use, but they joined heavily in cotton farming.

5. Pickrell, *Pioneer Women in Texas,* p. 181–82.

6. Ibid., p. 60.

7. J. Taylor Allen, *Early Pioneer Days in Texas,* p. 4; T. U. Taylor, "A Frontier Home"; Hall, *Surviving on the Texas Frontier* (forthcoming).

8. Hall, *Surviving on the Texas Frontier,* p. 6; Taylor, "A Frontier Home," pp. 112–13; "Tragedy and Comedy of Comanche County as Seen by Mrs. Greene," Nannie Greene Little Scrapbook, p. 49.

9. Steinfeldt, "Nineteenth Century Textiles," p. 6.

10. Carrington, *Women in Early Texas,* p. 259; see Holman and Persons, *Buckskin and Homespun,* p. 30. They indicate that mohair was brought to Hays County in 1857 from South Carolina. However, a cotton-and-mohair coverlet produced by Polly Mayes in Hays County has been dated to 1849.

11. "Tragedy and Comedy of Comanche County."

12. J. Marvin Hunter, *Pioneer History of Bandera County: Seventy Five Years of Intrepid History,* p. 144; Ronnie C. Tyler and Lawrence R. Murphy, eds., *The Slave Narratives of Texas,* p. 35.

13. Diane Greene Taylor, "Preliminary Report on a Survey of Textiles Made and Used in Texas," pp. 5, 7.

14. Quoted in Gilbert Giddings Benjamin, *The Germans in Texas: A Study in Immigration,* p. 80; Allen, *Early Pioneer Days in Texas,* p. 5; Taylor, "A Frontier Home," pp. 112–13.

15. Pickrell, *Pioneer Women in Texas,* p. 472.

16. Quoted in Mrs. Goldsby Childers account, Pickrell, *Pioneer Women in Texas,* p. 322; Allen, *Early Pioneer Days in Texas,* p. 16.

17. "Tragedy and Comedy of Comanche County."

18. Hall, *Surviving on the Texas Frontier* (forthcoming). Hall was born in 1857, so her memories of girlhood focus on the 1860s and 1870s, but many of her observations are apt for any decade; even when their mothers worked with commercial cloth, young girls felt overwhelmed by the duties before them. Lucy Larcom remembered of her nineteenth-century New England girlhood scrutinizing the "many thousand, thousand stitches" in her father's coat and pantaloons and concluding, "I suppose I have got to grow up and have a husband, and put all those little stitches into *his* coats and pantaloons. Oh; I never, never can do it!" See Mirra Bank, *Anonymous Was a Woman,* p. 23.

19. Bureau of the Census, Census Records, 1850 and 1860.

20. Taylor, "Preliminary Report," p. 9.

21. Diane Greene Taylor, "Census Notes," Winedale, 1977.

22. Taylor, "Preliminary Report," p. 8.

23. Taylor, "Census Notes."

24. Pickrell, *Pioneer Women in Texas,* p. 156.

25. Ibid., p. 194.

26. Carrington, *Women in Early Texas,* p. 28; Allen, *Early Pioneer Days in Texas,* p. 76. I found no reference to the weaving of rag rugs, beyond the Sanctificationist enterprise mentioned in Chapter 4. According to Weissman and Lavitt, in *Labors of Love,* floor rugs (as opposed to "bed ruggs" and other furniture coverings) were a relatively late addition to European and American interiors, but rag rugs were increasingly produced and used in America in the nineteenth century. Carrington, in *Women in Early Texas,* did note of the Civil War era that rugs were created "of small scraps of material, either cotton or wool, hooked or looped onto sacking or burlap." One can surmise that because woven rag rugs required large amounts of fabric, frontier women rejected using their worn or new material in this way, instead finding more pressing needs for it.

27. Allen, *Early Pioneer Days in Texas,* pp. 112–13; Mills, *Calico Chronicle,* p. 23; Pickrell, *Pioneer Women in Texas,* p. 194.

28. Amzina Wade, "Recollections of a Child's Life on a Pioneer Plantation," *Chronicles of Smith County* 19, no. 2 (Winter, 1980): 60; W. Eugene Hollon and Ruth Lapham Butler, *William Bollaert's Texas,* p. 265 fn.

29. Holman and Persons, *Buckskin and Homespun,* pp. 42–43.

30. "Tragedy and Comedy of Comanche County."

31. Ibid.

32. Allen, *Early Pioneer Days in Texas,* p. 76; Rawick, "Texas Narratives, Part 1," p. 220.

33. See "Distribution of Slaves in Texas, 1837" and "Distribution of Slaves in Texas, 1858," maps following p. 212 in Elizabeth Silverthorne, *Plantation Life in Texas.*

34. Entry of Feb. 8, 1853, Julian Sidney Devereux Papers, Box 2N214, Center for American History.

35. See Abigail Curlee Holbrook, "A Glimpse of Life on Antebellum Slave Plantations in Texas," *Southwestern Historical Quarterly* 74 (Apr., 1973): 371–72.

36. Rawick, "Texas Narratives, Part 1," p. 292; Hollon and Butler, *William Bollaert's Texas,* p. 208.

37. Tyler and Murphy, *The Slave Narratives of Texas,* p. 42.

38. Ibid., pp. 37–38.

39. Ibid., p. 63.

40. Davis McAuley, "Slave Life and Work in Bastrop County," *Sayersville Historical Association Bulletin* 7 (Winter, 1986): 21.

41. See Fry, *Stitched from the Soul,* p. 49.

42. Parker, "Institute of Texas Cultures," p. 14.

43. Tyler and Murphy, *The Slave Narratives of Texas*, pp. 37–38, 42.

44. Parker, "Institute of Texas Cultures," p. 14.

45. Malone, *Women on the Texas Frontier*, p. 33; Fry, in *Stitched from the Soul*, demonstrates that nineteenth-century slave women quilters did develop a distinctive aesthetic based on their African roots and African-American identity, but quilting allows greater liberty in form and technique than does weaving.

46. Tyler and Murphy, *The Slave Narratives of Texas*, p. 63; Rawick, "Texas Narratives, Part 1," p. 462.

47. Malone, *Women on the Texas Frontier*, p. 36.

48. Randolph B. Campbell, *An Empire for Slavery: The Peculiar Institution in Texas*, p. 139; McAuley, "Slave Life and Work in Bastrop County," p. 22.

49. Holbrook, "A Glimpse of Life," p. 374; Hollon and Butler, *William Bollaert's Texas*, p. 272.

50. Silverthorne, *Plantation Life in Texas*, p. 99.

51. Ibid. In *Stitched from the Soul*, her study of slave textile production, Fry notes that slaves "learned how to use plant dyes expertly" (p. 44).

52. Fry, *Stitched from the Soul*, p. 82.

53. Comments on Lucy Bugg Kyle and Harriet Hamlin McDowell-Bolling in Pickrell, *Pioneer Women in Texas*, pp. 139, 356.

54. Carrington, *Women in Early Texas*, p. 259.

55. Fry, *Stitched from the Soul*, p. 31.

56. Pickrell, *Pioneer Women in Texas*, p. 406.

57. Hollon and Butler, *William Bollaert's Texas*, p. 272.

58. "'This Feeble Circle of Light.'"

59. Strasser, *Never Done*, p. 105. The first washing machine was patented in the United States in 1846, but Strasser notes, nineteenth-century machines "saved little time and not much labor" (p. 116). Few found their way to Texas in the mid–nineteenth century anyway; Fry, in *Stitched from the Soul*, concludes, "The process was time consuming, tedious, and extremely hard on textiles" (pp. 41–42).

60. Pickrell, *Pioneer Women in Texas*, p. 334.

61. Ibid., pp. 156, 182.

62. In part, the continued spinning would be a matter of habit and choice and, in part, a response to a lack of affordable knitting yarns. Note that the Harrison County slave factory of the late 1850s mentioned below offered "stocking yarns."

63. Mills, *Calico Chronicle*, p. 19.

64. Parker, "Institute of Texas Cultures," pp. 10–12, cites Michael Rugeley Moore's "The Texas Penitentiary and Textile Production in

the Civil War Era," Honors paper, HIS 679H, Sam Houston State University, Huntsville, Texas, 1984.

65. Holbrook, "A Glimpse of Life," p. 372.

66. Parker, "Institute of Texas Cultures," p. 11.

CHAPTER FOUR

1. Hunter, *Pioneer History of Bandera County,* p. 232.

2. Don H. Biggers, *German Pioneers in Texas,* p. 82; Ida Lasater Huckabay, *Ninety-Four Years in Jack County, 1854–1948,* p. 9.

3. Biggers, *German Pioneers in Texas,* p. 82. Fiedler reported, "We had ruined our brand new suits." His experience echoes that of Texas governor Francis Lubbock, who, clad in buckskin pants on an expedition hunting for hostile Indians in 1836, got drenched in a rainstorm, then "backed up to a hot mesquite fire." He had to ride "a day or two" with the pants rapidly shrinking, then "in a manner to cut them off my limbs." Lubbock concluded, "They are more entertaining in a picture or a romance than on one's shanks." See Steinfeldt, "Nineteenth Century Textiles," p. 13.

4. Hall, *Surviving on the Texas Frontier* (forthcoming).

5. Ibid., p. 11.

6. Ibid., p. 13. Hall could not learn to spin from her impatient mother; when her adored father stepped in and guided her, she learned quickly.

7. Ibid., p. 32.

8. Ibid., p. 34.

9. Ibid., pp. 50–51.

10. Fannie Davis Beck, *On the Texas Frontier: Autobiography of a Texas Pioneer,* pp. 27–28.

11. Ibid., p. 96.

12. See Robert W. Delaney, "Matamoras, Port for Texas during the Civil War," *Southwestern Historical Quarterly* 58 (Apr., 1955): 473.

13. Margaret Swett Henson's *The Cartwrights of San Augustine: Three Generations of Agrarian Entrepreneurs in Nineteenth-Century Texas,* p. 220, gives the $3 to $5 figure. Betty Mills in *Calico Chronicle,* p. 24, mentions calico at $4 to $5. Eugenia Haldeman Openheimer in "Sketch of Major Horrace Haldeman and Pioneer Days in Bell County," in *Proceedings of the Sixth Annual Reunion of the Old Settlers' Association of Bell County,* said her family paid as much as $10 a yard for calico and muslin, and Beck in *On the Texas Frontier* reported calico costing $25 a yard. The $24 dress is noted in Henson, p. 219.

14. Mary S. Estill, ed., "Diary of a Confederate Congressman, 1862–1863," *Southwestern Historical Quarterly* 39, no. 1 (July, 1935): 51. Sex-

ton also called the $2.50 a yard he paid for calico "Horrible, Horrible."

15. *Dallas Herald,* Nov. 29, 1862, p. 2 in Texas Newspaper Files, Center for American History.

16. Henson, *The Cartwrights of San Augustine,* p. 220.

17. See Estelle Hudson and Henry R. Maresh, *Czech Pioneers of the Southwest,* p. 63. It appears that the Czech emigrants in general did not possess or did not practice spinning and weaving skills; one, Josef Shiller, stated, "I do not recall that the Czechs or Germans wove any cloth, but the Anglo Saxons did"; letter of Aug. 18, 1864, Perry Papers.

18. Hudson and Maresh, *Czech Pioneers of the Southwest,* p. 106.

19. Ledbetter Papers, Center for American History, University of Texas at Austin.

20. Ralph Wooster, "Life in Civil War East Texas," *East Texas Historical Journal* 3, no. 2 (Oct., 1965): 96.

21. See Karen Gerhardt Britton, *Bale o' Cotton: The Mechanical Art of Cotton Ginning,* p. 45.

22. Mrs. A. D. Gentry, "Reminiscences of Mrs. J. J. Greenwood," *Frontier Times* 2, no. 3 (Dec., 1924): 12.

23. Henson, *The Cartwrights of San Augustine,* p. 220; Gentry, "Reminiscences of Mrs. J. J. Greenwood," p. 12.

24. Quoted in Jack Stoltz, "Kaufman County in the Civil War," *East Texas Historical Journal* 28, no. 1 (1990): 42; court record reproduced in Huckabay, *Ninety-Four Years in Jack County,* p. 92.

25. *Dallas Herald,* Nov. 19, 1862, p. 2, in Texas Newspaper Files.

26. Holman and Persons, *Buckskin and Homespun,* p. 43; Henson, *The Cartwrights of San Augustine,* p. 219.

27. Sallie Haltom, "My Life in Tarrant County and Other Parts of Texas," *Southwestern Historical Quarterly* 60 (July, 1956): 102; Henson, *The Cartwrights of San Augustine,* p. 232.

28. Letter of Jan. 11, 1863, Maverick Family Papers, Center for American History.

29. Holbrook, "A Glimpse of Life," p. 372.

30. Henson, *The Cartwrights of San Augustine,* p. 220.

31. Openheimer, "Sketch of Major Horrace Haldeman," p. 12; see "Lavaca County," in Taylor's "Statewide Textile Survey Files."

32. Notes in Ledbetter Papers, Center for American History.

33. Quoted in Holbrook, "A Glimpse of Life," p. 372.

34. Pickrell, *Pioneer Women in Texas,* p. 334.

35. Wade, "Recollections of a Child's Life," p. 46.

36. Oates, "Texas under the Secessionists," *Southwestern Historical Quarterly* 67 (Oct., 1963): 190–91. Oates notes that the committees collected, among other items, blankets, socks, pants, and shirts, but we

must recognize that women's efforts went first into producing these items.

37. Pickrell, *Pioneer Women in Texas,* pp. 200–202, 373.

38. Rawick, "Texas Narratives, Part 1," pp. 99–100.

39. Carrington, *Women in Early Texas,* p. 178.

40. Letter of May 18, 1862, Perry Papers.

41. Sallie Reynolds Matthews, *Interwoven,* p. 56.

42. "Spent Four Long Years in a Cave," *Frontier Times* 2, no. 7 (Apr., 1925): 5. My thanks to T. Lindsay Baker for bringing this item to my attention.

43. Haltom, "My Life in Tarrant County," p. 102; Carrington, *Women in Early Texas,* p. 165.

44. In Ledbetter Papers, Center for American History.

45. Carrington, *Women in Early Texas,* p. 225.

46. Holman and Persons, *Buckskin and Homespun,* p. 42.

47. Vera Lea Dugas, "Texas Industry, 1860–1880," *Southwestern Historical Quarterly* 59 (Oct., 1955): 157.

48. Wooster, "Life in Civil War East Texas," p. 96; in an example of relief efforts for soldiers' families, McLennan County records show that commissioners set aside $4000 to buy cloth to distribute for this purpose. See Tony E. Duty's "'The Home Front': McLennan County in the Civil War," *Texana* 12, no. 3 (1976): 216.

49. Parker, "Institute of Texas Cultures," p. 13.

50. Quoted in William W. White, "The Disintegration of an Army: Confederate Forces in Texas, April–June, 1865," *East Texas Historical Journal* 26, no. 2 (1988): 44.

51. Ralph Wooster, "Wealthy Texans, 1870," *Southwestern Historical Quarterly* 74 (July, 1970): 25–26. Wooster relates that merchants made up only 15.6 percent of the upper economic tier of Texans in 1860. In 1870, they comprised almost 40 percent; quoted in Mills, *Calico Chronicle,* p. 24.

52. Benjamin's *The Germans in Texas* relates that at the Comal Cotton Manufacturing Company "from 1865–1867 there were manufactured 160,000 yards of domestics, 35,000 Osnaburgs, and 35,000 pounds of yarn"; see Parker, "Institute of Texas Cultures," p. 11. The mills using Texas cotton exclusively were the Lone Star Mill Cotton Factory, the Eureka Manufacturing Company, and Houston City Mills.

53. Benjamin, *The Germans in Texas,* p. 70.

54. Gentry, "Reminiscences of Mrs. J. J. Greenwood," p. 13.

55. Frances Bramlette Farris, *From Rattlesnakes to Road Agents: Rough Times on the Frio,* p. 11. Of her mother, Louisa Thomas Bramlette, in Frio County, Farris wrote, "When Mother came west she brought her

old spinning wheel with her—the one she had used during the War between the States to make clothing for the family as well as for the boys who wore the gray. She never found much use for it after she arrived at her final home since she was unable to get cotton to spin her thread. When she had the opportunity, she traded the wheel for a fine, large female pig. . . ."

56. For example, in the Bowie County census, Ursele C. Matthews, a twenty-five-year-old white female from Arkansas was identified as "Weaver."

57. Diane Greene Taylor, "Preliminary Report of a Survey of Textiles Made and Used in Texas" (paper presented at the annual meeting of the Texas State Historical Association, 1977), pp. 3, 19.

58. Rev. C. C. White and Ada Morehead Holland, *No Quittin' Sense.*

59. Campbell Loughmiller and Lynn Loughmiller, eds., *Big Thicket Legacy,* pp. 7–8.

60. A student from a Norwegian family who immigrated to the Midwest in the nineteenth century once told me that her grandmother, on gaining access to commercial cloth, had her husband and sons drag her loom to a nearby gully and throw it in; Mary Reid, "Fashions of the Republic," *Southwestern Historical Quarterly* 45 (Jan., 1942): 244.

Bibliography

Allen, J. Taylor. *Early Pioneer Days in Texas.* Dallas: Wilkinson Printing Company, 1918.

Anders, David. "Typescript Reminiscences, 1897." Typescript, Center for American History, University of Texas, Austin, Texas.

Anderson, Kathy Jo. "Texas Migration and Immigration." Paper prepared for spring, 1994, American Frontier Women course, St. Edward's University, Austin, Texas.

Applegate, Jess. "Making Do in the Wilderness." In *Looking Far West: The Search for the American West in History, Myth, and Literature,* ed. Frank Bergon and Zeese Papanikolas. New York: New American Library, 1978.

Bachmann, Ingrid. "Poke Out Her Eyes: Tales of Favorite Family Fabrics." *Fiberarts* 20, no. 1 (Summer, 1993): 48–50.

Baker, Jean H. *Mary Todd Lincoln: A Biography.* New York: W. W. Norton & Company, 1987.

Bank, Mirra. *Anonymous Was a Woman.* New York: St. Martin's Press, 1979.

Beck, Fannie Davis [Veale]. *On the Texas Frontier: Autobiography of a Texas Pioneer.* St. Louis: Britt Printing and Publishing Company, 1937.

Benjamin, Gilbert Giddings. *The Germans in Texas: A Study in Immigration.* Austin: Jenkins Publishing Company, 1974.

Bergon, Frank, and Zeese Papanikolas, eds. *Looking Far West: The Search for the American West in History, Myth, and Literature.* New York: New American Library, 1978.

Biggers, Don H. *German Pioneers in Texas*. Fredericksburg, Tex.: Fredericksburg Publishing Company, 1925.

Bonta, Marcia. "Eliza Lucas Pinckney, Cultivator of Indigo." In *Dyes from Nature,* ed. Rita Buchanan, 33–36. New York: Brooklyn Botanic Garden, 1990.

Briggs, Rose T. "Plymouth Colony's Dye Plants." In *Dye Plants and Dyeing—A Handbook,* 92–94. Brooklyn: Brooklyn Botanic Garden, 1964.

Britton, Karen Gerhardt. *Bale o' Cotton: The Mechanical Art of Cotton Ginning.* College Station: Texas A&M University Press, 1992.

Buley, R. Carlyle. *The Old Northwest Pioneer Period, 1815–1840.* 2 vols. Indianapolis: Indiana Historical Society, 1950.

Bureau of the Census. Census Records, 1850 and 1860. Microfilm, Center for American History, University of Texas, Austin, Texas.

Campbell, Randolph B. *An Empire for Slavery: The Peculiar Institution in Texas, 1821–1865.* Baton Rouge: Louisiana State University Press, 1989.

Carrington, Evelyn M., ed. *Women in Early Texas.* Austin: Pemberton Press, 1975.

Clinton, Catherine. *The Plantation Mistress.* New York: Pantheon Books, 1982.

Coker, Lily. Telephone interview with author, May 26, 1994.

Cunningham, Patricia. "Elmey Sammis Trimmer, Tailoress and Weaver." In *Making the American Home: Middle-Class Women and Domestic Material Culture, 1840–1940,* ed. Marilyn Ferris Motz and Pat Browne. Bowling Green, Ohio: Bowling Green State University Popular Press, 1988.

Curlee, Abigail. "The History of a Texas Slave Plantation, 1831–63." *Southwestern Historical Quarterly* 26 (Oct., 1922): 79–127.

Daurelle, Jude. "A Place to Come To." *Piecework* 2, no. 3 (May/June, 1994): 8–12.

Delaney, Robert W. "Matamoras, Port for Texas during the Civil War." *Southwestern Historical Quarterly* 58 (Apr., 1955): 473–87.

Devereux, Julian Sidney. Papers. Center for American History, University of Texas, Austin, Texas.

Dugas, Vera Lea. "Texas Industry, 1860–1880." *Southwestern Historical Quarterly* 59 (Oct., 1955): 151–83.

Duty, Tony E. "'The Home Front': McLennan County in the Civil War." *Texana* 12, no. 3 (1976): 197–238.

Earle, Alice Morse. *Home Life in Colonial Days.* 1898. Reprint, Stockbridge, Mass.: Berkshire Traveller Press, 1974.

Edward, David B. *The History of Texas Or the Emigrant's, Farmer's & Politician's Guide to the Character, Climate, Soil & Productions of*

That Country. 1836. Reprint, Austin: Texas State Historical Association, 1990.

Estill, Mary S., ed. "Diary of a Confederate Congressman, 1862–1863." *Southwestern Historical Quarterly* 39, no. 1 (July, 1935): 33–65.

Evans, Sarah. *Born for Liberty*. New York: Free Press, 1991.

Everett, Dianna. *The Texas Cherokees: A People between Two Fires, 1819–1840*. Norman: University of Oklahoma Press, 1990.

Exley, Jo Ella Powell, ed. *Texas Tears and Texas Sunshine: Voices of Frontier Women*. College Station: Texas A&M University Press, 1985.

Faragher, John Mack. "The Midwestern Farming Family, 1850." In *Women's America: Refocusing the Past,* ed. Linda K. Kerber and Jane Sherron DeHart. New York: Oxford University Press, 1991.

Farris, Frances Bramlette. *From Rattlesnakes to Road Agents: Rough Times on the Frio*. Fort Worth: Texas Christian University Press, 1985.

Fenley, Florence. *Oldtimers: Frontier Days in Uvalde Section of South West Texas*. Uvalde: Hornsby Press, 1939.

Fox-Genovese, Elizabeth. *Within the Plantation Household: Black and White Women of the Old South*. Chapel Hill: University of North Carolina Press, 1988.

Fry, Gladys-Marie. *Stitched from the Soul: Slave Quilts from the Ante-Bellum South*. New York: Dutton Studio Books, 1990.

Gentry, Mrs. A. D. "Reminiscences of Mrs. J. J. Greenwood." *Frontier Times* 2, no. 3 (Dec., 1924): 12–13.

Goodrich, Frances Louisa. *Mountain Homespun*. 1931. Reprint, Knoxville: University of Tennessee Press, 1989.

Graham, Joe S., ed. *Hecho en Tejas: Texas-Mexican Folk Arts and Crafts*. Denton: University of North Texas Press, 1992.

Hall, Sarah Harkey. *Surviving on the Texas Frontier: The Journal of a Frontier Orphan Girl in San Saba County*. Austin: Eakin Press, forthcoming.

Haltom, Sallie. "My Life in Tarrant County and Other Parts of Texas." *Southwestern Historical Quarterly* 60 (July, 1956): 100–105.

Harris, Dilue. "The Reminiscences of Mrs. Dilue Harris." *Quarterly of the Texas State Historical Association* 4, no. 1 (July, 1900): 85–127.

Henson, Margaret Swett. *The Cartwrights of San Augustine: Three Generations of Agrarian Entrepreneurs in Nineteenth-Century Texas*. Austin: Texas State Historical Association, 1993.

Holbrook, Abigail Curlee. "A Glimpse of Life on Antebellum Slave Plantations in Texas." *Southwestern Historical Quarterly* 74 (Apr., 1973): 361–83.

Hollon, W. Eugene, and Ruth Lapham Butler. *William Bollaert's Texas*. Norman: University of Oklahoma Press, 1956.

Holman, David, and Billie Persons. *Buckskin and Homespun: Frontier Texas Clothing, 1820–1870*. Austin: Wind River Press, 1979.

Huckabay, Ida Lasater. *Ninety-Four Years in Jack County, 1854–1948*. 1949. Reprint, Waco, Tex.: Texian Press, 1979.

Hudson, Estelle, and Henry R. Maresh. *Czech Pioneers of the Southwest*. Dallas: South-West Press, 1934.

Hunter, J. Marvin. *Pioneer History of Bandera County: Seventy Five Years of Intrepid History*. Bandera: Hunter's Printing House, 1922.

Jenkins, Malinda. *Gambler's Wife: The Life of Malinda Jenkins*. Boston: Houghton Mifflin, 1933.

Jones, Ethel Frances. "The Elixir of Youth." *Boone County [Arkansas] Historian* 17, no. 1 (Jan./Feb./Mar., 1994): 5–10.

Jones, Jacqueline. *Labor of Love, Labor of Sorrow: Black Women, Work, and the Family from Slavery to the Present*. New York: Random House, 1985.

Jones, Marie Beth. *Peach Point Plantation: The First 150 Years*. Waco, Tex.: Texian Press, 1982.

Jordan, Terry G. *German Seed in Texas Soil: Immigrant Farmers in Nineteenth-Century Texas*. Austin: University of Texas Press, 1975.

Larkin, Jack. *The Reshaping of Everyday Life*. New York: Harper & Row, 1988.

Ledbetter, Lena Dancy. Papers. Center for American History, University of Texas, Austin, Texas.

Loughmiller, Campbell, and Lynn Loughmiller, eds. *Big Thicket Legacy*. Austin: University of Texas Press, 1977.

McAuley, Davis. "Slave Life and Work in Bastrop County." *Sayersville Historical Association Bulletin* 7 (Winter, 1986): 17–25.

McMillen, Sally J. *Southern Women: Black and White in the Old South*. Arlington Heights, Ill.: Harlan Davidson, 1992.

MacDonald, Anne L. *No Idle Hands: The Social History of American Knitting*. New York: Ballantine Books, 1988.

Malone, Ann Patton. *Women on the Texas Frontier: A Cross-Cultural Perspective*. El Paso: Texas Western Press, 1983.

Marks, Paula Mitchell. *Turn Your Eyes toward Texas: Pioneers Sam and Mary Maverick*. College Station: Texas A&M Press, 1989.

Matthews, Sallie Reynolds. *Interwoven*. Houston: Anson Jones Press, 1936.

Maverick, Mary. Family Papers. Center for American History, University of Texas, Austin, Texas.

Mills, Betty J. *Calico Chronicle*. Lubbock: Texas Tech Press, 1985.

Milner, Clyde A., II, ed. "Kitturah Belknap Prepares for the Trip to Oregon, 1847–1848." In *Major Problems in the History of the Ameri-*

can West: Documents and Essays. Lexington, Mass.: D. C. Heath and Company, 1989.

Oates, Stephen B. "Texas under the Secessionists." *Southwestern Historical Quarterly* 67 (Oct., 1963): 167–212.

Openheimer, Eugenia Haldeman. "Sketch of Major Horrace Haldeman and Pioneer Days in Bell County." In *Proceedings of the Sixth Annual Reunion of the Old Settlers' Association of Bell County*. N.p., [1904].

Parker, Jane. "Institute of Texan Cultures Final Report, Summer, 1988— Early Texas Textiles."

Perry, James Franklin, Stephen Samuel Perry Sr., and James Franklin Perry Jr. Papers. Center for American History, University of Texas, Austin, Texas.

Pickrell, Annie Doom, ed. *Pioneer Women in Texas*. 1929. Reprint, Austin: Pemberton Press, 1970.

Price, Dona. Personal notes provided to author, June 11, 1994.

Ragsdale, Crystal Sasse, ed. *The Golden Free Land: The Reminiscences and Letters of Women on an American Frontier*. Austin: Landmark Press, 1976.

Rawick, George P., ed. "Texas Slave Narratives, Part 1." In *The American Slave: A Composite Autobiography*. Westport, Conn.: Greenwood Press, 1979.

Redding, Debbie. *Learning to Weave with Debbie Redding*. Loveland, Col.: Interweave Press, 1984.

Reid, Mary. "Fashions of the Republic." *Southwestern Historical Quarterly* 45 (Jan., 1942): 244–54.

Robison, E. Jane, and Jeri Robison-Turner, eds. *Unbroken Circle*. Austin: Plain View Press, 1986.

San Antonio Bicentennial Heritage Committee. *San Antonio in the Eighteenth Century*. San Antonio: Clarke Printing Company, 1976.

Sayer, Chloe. *Arts and Crafts of Mexico*. San Francisco: Chronicle Books, 1990.

Seele, Hermann. *The Cypress and Other Writings of a German Pioneer in Texas*. Trans. Edward C. Breitenkamp. Austin: University of Texas Press, 1979.

Shipman, Daniel. *Frontier Life: 58 Years in Texas*. N.p., 1879.

Silverthorne, Elizabeth. *Plantation Life in Texas*. College Station: Texas A&M University Press, 1986.

Smithwick, Noah. *The Evolution of a State or Recollections of Old Texas Days*. 1900. Reprint, Austin: University of Texas Press, 1984.

"Spent Four Long Years in a Cave." *Frontier Times* 2, no. 7 (Apr., 1925): 4–5.

Spruill, Julia Cherry. *Women's Life and Work in the Southern Colonies.* 1938. Reprint, New York: W. W. Norton & Company, 1972.

Steen, Mary Frost. "To Utilize Every Idle Hand: Silk Culture in the United States." *Spin-Off* 18, no. 2 (Summer, 1994): 104–110.

Steinfeldt, Cecilia. "Nineteenth Century Textiles in Texas." Paper presented to the Brazos Historical Society, 1984.

———, and Donald L. Stover. *Early Texas Furniture and Decorative Arts.* San Antonio: Trinity University Press, 1973.

Stoltz, Jack. "Kaufman County in the Civil War." *East Texas Historical Journal* 28, no. 1 (1990): 37–44.

Strasser, Susan. *Never Done: A History of American Housework.* New York: Pantheon Books, 1982.

Strickler, Carol. *American Woven Coverlets.* Loveland, Col.: Interweave Press, 1987.

Taylor, Diane Greene. "Census Notes," Winedale Historical Center, Winedale, Tex., 1977.

———. "Preliminary Report on a Survey of Textiles Made and Used in Texas." Paper presented at the annual meeting of the Texas State Historical Association, 1977.

———. "Statewide Textile Survey Files," Winedale Historical Center, Winedale, Tex., 1977.

Taylor, T. U. "A Frontier Home." Typescript, in George F. Atkinson Papers, Texas Historical Survey [1935?], Center for American History, University of Texas, Austin, Texas.

Texas Newspaper Files, Center for American History, University of Texas, Austin, Texas.

"'This Feeble Circle of Light': Lighting Devices in Nineteenth Century Texas." *Star of the Republic Museum Notes* 15, no. 3 (Spring, 1991).

"Tragedy and Comedy of Comanche County as Seen by Mrs. Greene." Newspaper clipping, Nannie Greene Little Scrapbook, vol. 10, p. 49. Comanche Public Library, Comanche, Texas.

Trechsel, Gail Andrews. "Mourning Quilts: That Distress, By Industry, May Be Removed." *Piecework* 2, no. 2 (Mar./Apr., 1994): 52–57.

Tull, Delena. *A Practical Guide to Edible and Useful Plants.* Austin: Texas Monthly Press, 1987.

Tyler, Ronnie C., and Lawrence R. Murphy, eds. *The Slave Narratives of Texas.* Austin: Encino Press, 1974.

Ulrich, Laurel Thatcher. *Good Wives: Image and Reality in the Lives of Women in Northern New England, 1650–1750.* New York: Vintage Books, 1991.

———. *A Midwife's Tale: The Life of Martha Ballard Based on Her Diary, 1785–1812.* New York: Alfred A. Knopf, 1990.

Van Wagenen, Jared, Jr. *The Golden Age of Homespun*. Ithaca, N.Y.: Cornell University Press, 1953.

Vlach, John Michael. "Afro-American Folk Crafts in Nineteenth Century Texas." *Western Folklore* 40, no. 2 (Apr., 1981): 149–61.

Wade, Amzina. "Recollections of a Child's Life on a Pioneer Plantation." *Chronicles of Smith County* 19, no. 2 (Winter, 1980): 45–62.

Walker, Olive Todd. "Esther Amanda Sherrill Cullins: A Pioneer Woman of the Texas Frontier." *Southwestern Historical Quarterly* 47 (Jan., 1944): 234–49.

Weissman, Judith Reiter, and Wendy Lavitt. *Labors of Love: America's Textiles and Needlework, 1650–1930*. New York: Knopf, 1987.

White, Rev. C. C., and Ada Morehead Holland. *No Quittin' Sense*. Austin: University of Texas Press, 1994.

White, William W. "The Disintegration of an Army: Confederate Forces in Texas, April-June, 1865." *East Texas Historical Journal* 26, no. 2 (1988): 40–47.

Wooster, Ralph. "Life in Civil War East Texas." *East Texas Historical Journal* 3, no. 2 (October, 1965): 93–102.

———. "Wealthy Texans, 1870." *Southwestern Historical Quarterly* 74 (July, 1970): 24–35.

Index

Note: Pages with illustrations are indicated by **boldface** type.